# COLLECTIVE BARGAINING
# IN AFRICAN COUNTRIES

INTERNATIONAL INSTITUTE FOR LABOUR STUDIES

# COLLECTIVE BARGAINING IN AFRICAN COUNTRIES

BY

## B. C. ROBERTS

AND

## L. GREYFIÉ DE BELLECOMBE

MACMILLAN

London · Melbourne · Toronto

ST MARTIN'S PRESS

New York

1967

MACMILLAN AND COMPANY LIMITED
*Little Essex Street London WC2*
*also Bombay Calcutta Madras Melbourne*

THE MACMILLAN COMPANY OF CANADA LIMITED
*70 Bond Street Toronto 2*

ST MARTIN'S PRESS INC
*175 Fifth Avenue New York NY 10010*

Library of Congress catalog card no. 67-14192

PRINTED IN GREAT BRITAIN

# CONTENTS

|  |  | PAGE |
|---|---|---|
| INTRODUCTION |  | vii |

CHAP.

1. THE AREAS OF EMPLOYMENT COVERED BY COLLECTIVE
   AGREEMENTS — 1
   The Employed Labour Force : Size and Distribution — 1
   Skilled Workers — 5
   Racial Composition — 7
   The Coverage of Collective Agreements — 8
   In the French-speaking countries — 9
   In the English-speaking countries — 16

2. THE TRADE UNIONS — 24
   Trade Union Structure and Collective Bargaining in
   English-speaking countries — 25
   Trade Union Structure and Collective Bargaining in the
   French-speaking countries — 27
   The Strength of the Unions — 30

3. THE EMPLOYERS — 36
   Governments as Employers — 37
   The Private Employer — 40
   Employers' Associations — 41

4. COLLECTIVE BARGAINING — 46
   I. Collective Bargaining in English-speaking countries — 48
   The Recognition of Trade Unions — 49
   The Level of Negotiations — 53
   The Bargaining Machinery — 55
   The Settlement of Disputes arising in the Process of
   Negotiations — 61

   II. Collective Bargaining in the French-speaking
   countries — 68
   Collective Bargaining and the Labour Code of 1952 — 68
   The Legislative Evolution since Independence — 73
   Theory and Practice — 76

v

CHAP.                                                       PAGE

5. THE CONTENT OF COLLECTIVE AGREEMENTS     81
   The Exercise of Trade Union Rights     83
   Legal Aspects of the Employment Relationship     89
      Conclusion and Implementation of the Contract of
         Employment     89
      Suspension of the Contract of Employment     93
      Termination of Employment     94
   Wages and Related Benefits     98
   Social Benefits     106
   Hours of Work and Holidays     110

6. THE IMPLEMENTATION OF COLLECTIVE AGREEMENTS     113
   The Group of People concerned : Contracting and Non-
      contracting Parties     114
   Duration of the Agreements     117
   Effects and Sanction of Collective Agreements     119
   Grievances arising from the Implementation of Collective
      Agreements     123

APPENDIX I.    Kenya Industrial Relations Charter     131
APPENDIX II.    Extracts from the Labour Code, Republic     138
         of Senegal
APPENDIX III.    List of Legal Texts Published in the ILO
         Legislative Series     153

INDEX     155

# INTRODUCTION

WHENEVER men and women are employed it is necessary to establish the terms and conditions of their employment. The way that this is achieved may be by the unilateral decision of the employer, or by a personal agreement between the individual worker and the employer, or by a collective agreement between a group of workers organised in a trade union and the employer or a group of employers, or by the State through some kind of legislated arrangement, or by some combination of these various methods. In this study we are concerned primarily with the extent to which in African countries south of the Sahara, excluding South Africa, the terms and conditions of employment are regulated by collective agreements. We are interested in the other methods only in so far as they have a bearing upon the process of making collective agreements, and upon their contents.

In the classical model of industrial relations historically developed first in Britain, collective agreements are the outcome of negotiations between autonomous trade unions, representing all, or a group of workers and one or more equally autonomous employers.[1] In this classical model there are the minimum of outside constraints on either party — each is free to settle by the process of collective bargaining on the best terms he can obtain and to strike or lockout if negotiations reach a deadlock.

At the other end of the continuum from the pure collective bargaining model is the administrative model developed in the U.S.S.R. and other countries with fully planned economies. In this model collective agreements are not the outcome of a bargaining process between autonomous trade unions and employers, but the result of an administrative process of reconciliation between the interests of subordinate agencies of the State and the requirements of the State plan. The primary function of the collective agreement is to make clear and specific the rights and duties of workers and managers in achieving the common goal set forth in the State plans for the enterprise, the sector of industry concerned, and the economy as a whole.[2] Thus the nature and significance of the collective

---

[1] The first and still perhaps the most illuminating analysis of the British system of industrial relations was made by S. and B. Webb, *Industrial Democracy*, Longmans, 1897. See also E. H. Phelps Brown, *The Growth of British Industrial Relations*, Macmillan, 1959.

[2] See N. G. Aleksandrov, Soviet Labour Law (translation from Russian, Delhi, 1961).

vii

agreement in this model are determined primarily by the goals of the planning process, rather than by the outcome of bargaining between autonomous bodies in the environment of a market which continuously adjusts the supply price of labour to demand.

The two models at either extreme are no longer to be found in their absolutely pure form in either Britain or the Soviet Union. In both countries there has been a tendency to shift to a more intermediate position. While in Britain collective agreements are primarily the outcome of a collective bargaining process between autonomous bodies, the State has assumed an increasingly important role in determining basic conditions of employment and in assisting the parties to arrive at an agreement that satisfies the interest of the public as well as of themselves. In the Soviet Union it is clear that the situation in the labour market, more especially since the freedom of movement between jobs has been restored, cannot be ignored when collective agreements are being made : thus even under the conditions of prescriptive planning existing in the Communist countries there is a degree of locally negotiated adjustment, although a serious collective conflict between a trade union and the State is in theory and practice inadmissible.

Modification of the classic British model of collective bargaining has been carried a considerable distance by many countries inheriting this tradition, for example in the U.S.A. by the imposition of legislated constraints and obligations on the parties designed to alter the distribution of bargaining power so as to bring about a better balance and a more equitable agreement. In the case of Australia the right to strike and lockout, which has been regarded as an essential condition of the classical model, has been largely superseded by a quasi-judicial process of arbitration as the final stage of the collective bargaining method of arriving at a collective agreement.[1]

The system of industrial relations established by the British Government in its colonial territories in Africa was essentially the same as the classic model developed in Britain. However, while the same basic principles were followed, important modifications were made to meet the requirements of local conditions. Since independence the process of modification has been taken further and in most countries the trend has been in the direction of a more regulated system of collective bargaining.

In the French model, which lies between but closer to the British

---

[1] Many industrial stoppages occur in spite of the prohibition and a good number are in violation of the law.

than the Soviet model, a collective agreement is primarily a method of supplementing the basic terms and conditions of employment laid down in a legal code.[1] The bargaining process, which in France is between autonomous trade unions and employers, is carried out in the French-speaking countries of Africa under the guidance of an Inspecteur du Travail representing the State. Thus the system, as developed in these countries, which is a tripartite one that involves the participation of the State at every stage in the process of bargaining between employers and trade unions, has acquired something of the character of an administrative procedure. As in France, the terms of the collective agreement are essentially supplementary to the legally determined basic wage and conditions of employment laid down in the *Code du Travail*. Since independence the trend has been in the direction of a greater degree of legal regulation.

## THE PRECONDITIONS FOR THE DEVELOPMENT OF A COLLECTIVE BARGAINING SYSTEM

Before considering further the extent to which the terms and conditions of employment are determined in African countries by methods that may be classified as the same or similar to the basic models outlined above it is necessary to say a little about the conditions that must be fulfilled in the first instance. In a society where the number of persons employed is very small and where those who are employed for wages work on farms, in domestic households and for petty traders, there is little opportunity for collective bargaining to take place. Under these conditions the contracts of employment will be settled by personal negotiation on an individual basis. This situation only changes as the size of the employed labour force becomes substantial and relatively large numbers of workers are employed by public authorities and private enterprises in a wide range of productive activities. When economic development has reached this point the employed labour force will have become structured in a number of clearly identifiable categories. At the same time the units of employment are likely to include many that have grown to a size that has destroyed the personal relationship between employers and workers that is a characteristic feature of the small-scale

[2] See J.-D. Reynaud, *Les Syndicats en France*, Amand Colin, 1963. F. Sellier, *Stratégie de la lutte sociale, France 1936-1960*, Coll. Relations sociales, Les Éditions Ouvrières, 1961.

enterprise. When this stage has been reached it is administratively convenient and economically efficient for management to establish standards of wages and working conditions that are more common to whole categories of employees than to individuals, since this enables them to pursue a uniform hiring policy, to control and predict labour costs and to minimise personal conflicts over the wages of workers engaged on common tasks. These conditions equally provide employees with an opportunity and a stimulus to combine and present a common front to the employer, compelling him to negotiate the terms and conditions of employment collectively with the workers concerned instead of presenting them with a unilateral decision.

The creation of an employed labour force is thus the first condition that must be satisfied before there can be any collectively determined conditions of employment and we examine the extent to which this has come about in the African countries under survey in Chapter 1. An attempt is also made to indicate from information supplied by employers, unions and governments, the extent to which the various broad categories of the employed wage earners are covered by collective agreements. The evidence suggests that a stage has now been reached when the wages and working conditions of a substantial proportion of the employed wage-earning population are determined or considerably influenced by this method.

## THE DEVELOPMENT OF TRADE UNIONS AND EMPLOYERS' ORGANISATIONS

Whether the system of industrial relations is closer to the classical collective bargaining model or to the administrative model, trade unions are a factor of key importance. In the classical model trade unions must be capable of bringing effective pressure to bear upon employers in order to secure satisfactory agreements; in the administrative model they must be capable of representing workers and of assisting in the administration of the agreement after it has been reached and given legal effect. Trade unions that correspond to these requirements now exist in all of the countries that have been surveyed in this study. It is, of course, abundantly apparent that in size, structure and power, there are considerable differences between unions in the various countries concerned.

The pattern of union organisation in the former French territories was modelled on that which prevailed in France. This means that the unions in these countries are generally established on a broad industrial or occupational basis and have an allegiance to political or religious movements. But there have been changes since independence and there is a strong centripetal tendency. In Mali, for example, there is now a single union, that is more or less under State control. Elsewhere, a similar process of unification and the establishment of a close identity with the political party in power is taking place.

Trade unions in the former British territories have been just as greatly influenced by ideas of organisation and behaviour imported from the United Kingdom. Other influences have also been at work and the patterns of union organisation are perhaps less uniform than in the former French territories. Throughout the English-speaking territories there are many unions whose organisation is based upon the enterprise, but there are also a good number of large, well organised industry-wide, or broad occupational group unions. For example, in Zambia the African Mineworkers' Union is especially strong in the copper mining industry ; the Nigerian Teachers' Union might be cited as another example or the Railway African Workers' Union in Kenya. In both East and West Africa plantation workers are reasonably well organised and their unions have proved capable, with some assistance from the Plantation Workers' International and trade union movements of Britain and America, of negotiating industry-wide agreements of a comprehensive and advanced type.

The same trends towards centralisation and political control are also observable in the English-speaking territories as in the French, but local organisation is generally much stronger. In Ghana the trade union movement was transformed by political fiat from a multiplicity of tiny and often weak organisations into a group of 16 large unions organically linked to a strong central body firmly under the control of the Government. In Tanzania, since independence all the unions have been amalgamated into one national Tanzania Workers' Union. The trade union movements in the other English-speaking countries have not been radically reorganised as yet, but the tendency towards stronger central authority is evident in all of them except perhaps Nigeria. The problems of union organisation and their capacity to negotiate and bargain effectively are analysed in Chapter 2.

The growth of unions was a challenge to employers whose first response was hostility. Their behaviour, in this respect, was no different from that of employers in the older industrial countries.

In due course they came to terms with the unions, as they had also done in Europe, America and elsewhere. Unions were recognised and negotiating procedures were established. This development, which is described in Chapter 3, was helped in the British territories by the policy, strongly pursued by the British Government, of encouraging collective bargaining as the most appropriate way of determining wages and working conditions. The *Code du Travail* of 1952 gave similar encouragement, though implemented in a different way, to the growth of unions and the development of collective bargaining in the French territories.

In the English-speaking countries the large private employers, in particular the big international companies, have given a lead in the development of collective bargaining. They have introduced modern methods of personnel management and have sought to assist the trade unions with whom they negotiate to achieve stability by conceding the 'check-off' and providing facilities for union representatives to maintain close contact with their members.

Employers' organisations have been formed in most of the English-speaking countries and these have played an important role in helping employers to develop positive industrial relations policies. Most of these associations have affiliated to the Organisation of Employers' Federations and Employers in Developing Countries; this body has done a great deal to persuade employers to adopt an enlightened attitude through its advisory services. In the French-speaking countries employers' associations are much less important today than they were before independence when, in keeping with the highly centralised administration of the French overseas territories, they were controlled from France.

The most important employer in most of the countries is the State, if both the direct employees of central and local government and public enterprises and services are taken into account. In their initial response to trade unions, governments showed the same reluctance as private employers to enter into collective bargaining arrangements, but this attitude was incompatible with the support they were giving to the development of unions and they were compelled to abandon it in favour of recognising unions and listening to their claims.[1]

As employers, governments have special responsibilities, but they

[1] For an account of the evolution of the British Government's policy see B. C. Roberts, *Labour in the Tropical Territories of the Commonwealth*. G. Bell, London, 1964.

also face peculiar difficulties. On the one hand they are under pressure to behave as model employers, on the other they are responsible for the achievement of national economic goals. They must constantly bear in mind that concessions to unions have to be paid for in higher taxes, that pay increases in the public sector will be matched by pay increases in the private sector and if these increases in total are higher than the rate of real growth the effect on the economy will be inflationary. Thus governments, whatever the type of economic system, have tended to pursue a cautious wage policy. Since African countries have attained their independence, governments have shown, in their concern not to jeopardise the achievement of a higher rate of economic growth, a readiness to curb the demands of all unions for higher pay and of unions of government employees in particular, sometimes to the point of provoking considerable unrest.

A particular problem facing unions and governments is the exercise of the right to strike. Civil servants have the right to strike in Britain and they frequently exercise that right in France, but in many countries government employees do not have the right to strike. The situation in the African countries is complex. Most countries seek to prevent civil servants and the employees of critical public services such as light and power, water and health, from going on strike either by outright prohibition or the danger of incurring serious penalties. Where strikes have occurred in the English-speaking countries they have led in the past to Commissions of Inquiry and this has proved a reasonably effective way of resolving a difficult situation.

In spite of these limitations, employees in the public service, either working directly for the national or local government or in publicly-owned undertakings, are fairly highly organised in both English- and French-speaking countries. While there is a feeling in the unions that the limitations imposed upon their freedom to bargain are too great, the relationship between governments and unions is generally good ; and though acceptable compromises are sometimes difficult to work out, so far cataclysmic upheavals have been avoided with a certain degree of outside help.

## THE PROCESS OF COLLECTIVE BARGAINING

The right to determine the terms and conditions of employment by negotiating a collective agreement between unions and employers is accepted in all of the countries in Africa which have been the subject of this survey. But there are considerable differences between countries in the way in which the principle of collective bargaining is interpreted, as revealed by the evidence presented in Chapter 4.

Before bargaining can take place independent trade unions must exist and be recognised, but it hardly needs to be said that the formal recognition of a union is only the first step in the development of an effective collective bargaining system. In the early stages of collective bargaining the task of union leaders was made difficult by the refusal of employers to grant them ready access to their members. In many agreements in the English-speaking countries access is now specifically guaranteed under defined conditions. Special provision is now often made to allow local union officers to have leave to attend meetings and conferences, including longer periods of travel overseas. In this respect union officers are often much more generously treated than is normally the case in the United Kingdom and other advanced industrial countries. In the French-speaking countries, union recognition, access to members and the right of members and officers to participate in union activities are guaranteed by the labour codes, and extended through collective agreements in particular instances.

In the English-speaking countries legislation, following the British tradition, confined the power of the State to regulate the pattern of negotiations between unions and employers to the situation where they were unable to arrive at a voluntary agreement ; whereas in the French-speaking countries the law laid down the procedure to be followed and gave the representative of the State an important role in the conduct of negotiations.

Differences in the character of the legal framework, the type of trade unionism and general approach to industrial relations has produced a markedly different pattern in the procedures of collective bargaining in the English- and French-speaking countries.

In the English-speaking countries the collective bargaining process is widely varied. As in Britain, agreements may be negotiated at the level of the enterprise for a given occupational group, or at the national level for an entire industry and covering all categories of employees. Following British practice, unions and employers have set up by voluntary agreement joint negotiating committees and joint industrial councils. In addition to this type of formal negotiating machinery, there is a variety of supplemental arrangements including joint consultative committees and legally established minimum wage boards with statutory powers. Agreements may follow lengthy negotiations and highly formalised procedures, or be no more than a verbal undertaking by management, after informal discussions, on the basis of an *ad hoc* claim made by a union or the representative of a group of workers.

In the French-speaking countries the procedure is more standardised and more formal. A collective agreement is normally discussed in a Commission which consists not only of representatives of the employers and the unions but also of the Ministry of Labour. Unlike the situation in the British case, where the discussion will almost always be based upon a claim made by a union, the initiative and the substantive proposals will frequently come from the representative of the Ministry of Labour. In these circumstances, and further since the agreement is set in the context of a wide ranging system of legal regulation, it has as much of the character of an administrative regulation as it has of a collective bargain. Moreover, the agreement generally covers a whole section of industry and all categories of employees in that section though there may be supplementary agreements to cover special groups and particular areas of employment.

The system of voluntary negotiation developed in the various countries of Africa has permitted a good deal of flexibility in the methods and machinery for settling disputes. During the period of British rule all countries permitted workers to strike or employers to lockout, as a last resort if negotiations reached a complete deadlock. In every country an exception was made in the case of essential industries, such as water, electricity, health and sanitary services and police. Since independence, several countries have found it desirable to provide for the compulsory arbitration of any dispute in which a stoppage of work is threatened that is deemed by the Minister of Labour to be dangerous to the public interest. Before this stage is reached, however, there is ample opportunity for the parties to arrive at a voluntary settlement. In this respect all countries have developed conciliation services modelled on the British pattern. The Labour Commissioner generally has no power to intervene in the negotiations between unions and employers unless asked to do so by one or both of the parties. It is, however, part of the duty of the Ministry of Labour to keep in close touch with negotiations and to know when to offer discreet advice and the official services of a conciliator. When the official machinery has been exhausted and conciliation has failed, arbitration may be offered for voluntary acceptance or, in the minority of cases, may be imposed.

In the French-speaking countries the role of the Ministry of Labour is more influential in shaping the context of a collective agreement. Compulsory arbitration is the last resort of many countries, but in practice the great majority of disputes arising out of the negotiation and implementation of a collective agreement are settled by conciliation. Thus the trend towards a more centrally controlled system of industrial relations has not produced any startling shift in the method of negotiation or the settlement of conflicts. As in the British procedure, the Minister of Labour has to make certain that the conciliatory procedures have been exhausted before resort is made to compulsory arbitration.

Thus it is fair to say that while the trend in the English-speaking and non-English-speaking countries is in the direction of greater regulation and more government interference in connection with the exercise of the right to strike there is still a good deal of room for voluntary discussion and the autonomous negotiation of agreements. In the English-speaking countries, including those that have introduced authoritarian means of controlling unions and collective bargaining, there is a good deal of genuine free negotiation and the bulk of agreements are negotiated without outside interference.

## THE SCOPE AND CONTENT OF COLLECTIVE AGREEMENTS

The content of collective agreements naturally varies greatly in African countries as it varies greatly in the industrially more advanced countries of the world. At one end of the scale the scope of agreements is extremely limited, at the other it ranges over as wide an area as the most advanced agreements concluded in Europe or the United States.

There are important differences in the content of collective agreements that stem from differences in the basic systems of industrial relations that have been developed in the English- and French-speaking countries of Africa. Agreements in the French-speaking countries tend to be more uniform in their content, one might even say standardised, than is the case in the English-speaking countries. There are, however, a good many supplementary agreements and annexes that make for differences in detail.

From an examination of a large number of collective agreements from all the countries, it is possible to group the subject matter analysed in Chapter 5 into six main groups:

(1) Union recognition; union security provisions, including the 'check-off' system; access to members employed on plantations, in mines, factories or other places of employment; rights and duties of shop stewards; workplace meetings.

(2) Terms of employment; seniority provisions; lay-off procedures; severance payments; apprenticeship and training provisions.

(3) Wage scales; piece-rates; bonuses; overtime and shift premiums; other types of special payments.

(4) Hours of work; public holidays; vacations; maternity and other types of special leave.

(5) Safety provisions, including protective clothing or other items; welfare and other types of amenity, including good housing and medical services.

(6) Duration of the agreement; procedure for termination and amendment; implementation and interpretation procedures.

Not all of this range of items are necessarily to be found in any one agreement. It is, for example, not unusual for procedural matters to be covered by a separate agreement. However, many of these matters are covered in the more ambitious agreements negotiated between the large international companies and the unions.

In many agreements in the English-speaking countries there is a preamble in which the parties declare their interest in the development of good industrial relations and their intention to implement the agreement in this spirit. To this end there has been an endeavour, fostered by labour departments and supported by a number of employers, to promote joint consultative committees as an adjunct to collective bargaining. In some cases, for example in Kenya and Zambia, joint consultative committees were promoted on a fairly widespread scale before unions had been properly established, as a means of providing some experience of orderly committee procedures and a balanced discussion of issues.

It is frequently suggested that the promotion of collective bargaining as a method of determining the terms and conditions of employment of workers in Africa was a foolish error on the part of the former British and French Governments. The ILO and such trade union organisations as the International Confederation of Free Trade

Unions and the trade union centres of Britain, Scandinavia and the U.S.A. are severely criticised for perpetuating the error.[1] The fact that many of the countries, since gaining their independence, have introduced a greater degree of administrative regulation of collective bargaining may be cited as evidence of the inadequacy of the classical model of industrial relations for the countries of Africa. The first argument against the suitability of the collective bargaining model rests upon the contention that unions in Africa are too weak to bargain effectively and therefore it is socially undesirable to leave the standards of employment to be established by all-powerful and, by implication, ruthless employers.[2] The second argument that is advanced, often at the same time as the first though they are mutually contradictory, is that collective bargaining will lead to an unfair advantage being gained by organised workers and that the gains will create inflation, undermine economic stability and reduce the rate of economic growth.[3]

There is undoubtedly some truth in both of these arguments, but to provide definitive proof of the extent to which they are valid would require far more evidence than is at present available in most of the countries examined in this survey. But it has been possible to give an idea of (1) the workers covered by collective agreements ; (2) the effectiveness of union bargaining ; (3) the behaviour of employers ; (4) the actual pattern and process of the collective bargaining ; (5) the scope and contents of collective agreements in existence ; and (6) the implementation of the agreements. Together this indicates that collective agreements have become established as an important element in the industrial relations systems of the countries surveyed. The pattern of collective bargaining varies widely. At one level it bears close comparison with the situation in Britain and France, at another it is subordinate to the administrative authority and bears a closer resemblance to the position it occupies in the countries following a Communist system of government. Future development and the ultimate role of collective bargaining and collective agreements will depend upon the rate of economic growth and political theory and practice adopted in each country.

[1] See H. A. Turner, *Wage Trends, Wage Policies and Collective Bargaining: the Problems for Underdeveloped Countries*, Cambridge University Press, 1965.
[2] See F. T. de Vyver, 'The Transplantation of Trade Unionism to British Colonial Africa', Duke University Commonwealth-Studies Centre, April 1962.
[3] The argument is well stated by Turner, *op. cit.* p. 39.

Chapter 1

# THE AREAS OF EMPLOYMENT COVERED BY COLLECTIVE AGREEMENTS

## THE EMPLOYED LABOUR FORCE: SIZE AND DISTRIBUTION

IN most of the countries covered by this survey of collective agreements, the proportion of the labour force employed for wages and salaries is relatively low by comparison with the industrially advanced countries. At the time of writing the proportion of the population that depends mainly upon wages and salaries is, in a good number of the countries, less than 10 per cent of the total labour force ; only in a small minority of instances does the proportion exceed 50 per cent. Nevertheless, this section of the labour force is of special importance, since it is upon its activities that each country depends for the provision of its public services and for the production of every item other than food and a few simple hand-made products. No matter how significant self-employed primary producers might be — and in terms of their numbers they are quite clearly of the utmost economic and social importance — continued economic development and a rapid rate of economic growth depends mainly upon those who are in the wage and salaried groups of employees. Moreover, the numbers involved will gradually grow larger as economic development takes place.

There are considerable variations in the size of the labour force in the countries examined and also in the percentage of the labour force estimated to work for wages and salaries. The wide differences that exist are illustrated in the following table which is based upon material obtained from official surveys and upon estimates made by the Statistical Department of the ILO. It is necessary to emphasise that these figures are often no more than rough guesses at the approximate numbers in the years cited.[1]

[1] For a more detailed analysis of the statistics of the labour force and percentage of wage and salary earners, see K. C. Doctor and Hans Gallis, ' Size and Characteristics of Wage Employment in Africa : Some Statistical Estimates', *International Labour Review*, February 1966.

I

TABLE 1

| Country | Year | Population 000's | Labour Force 000's | Wage and Salary Earner 000's | % |
|---|---|---|---|---|---|
| **Central Africa** | | | | | |
| Angola | 1954/55 | — | 1,455 | 400 | 27·0 |
| Cameroon | 1962 | 3,000 | 1,764 | 100 | 5·6 |
| Chad | 1961 | 2,674 | 1,197 | 42 | 3·0 |
| Congo (Kinshasa) | 1955 | 13,650 | 6,199 | 1183 | 19·1 |
| Congo (Brazzaville) | 1960 | — | 450 | 50 | 11·1 |
| Gabon | 1963 | 500 | 220 | 44 | 20·0 |
| **East Africa** | | | | | |
| Ethiopia | 1960 | — | 7,494 | 500 | 6·7 |
| Kenya | 1961 | 7,000 | 3,029 | 620 | 20·5 |
| Malagasy Republic | 1961 | 5,000 | 2,550 | 206 | 8·0 |
| Malawi | 1961 | 3,000 | 860 | 140 | 16·3 |
| Mozambique | 1960 | — | 1,922 | 585 | 30·5 |
| Rhodesia (Southern) | 1962 | 4,000 | 1,280 | 700 | 54·7 |
| Tanzania | 1962 | 9,100 | 3,837 | 390 | 10·2 |
| Uganda | 1960 | 6,500 | 2,471 | 350 | 14·1 |
| Zambia | 1961 | 3,483 | 1,012 | 269 | 26·5 |
| **West Africa** | | | | | |
| Dahomey | 1961 | 1,800 | 933 | 36 | 3·9 |
| Central African Republic | 1961 | 1,100 | 550 | 47 | 8·5 |
| Ghana | 1960 | 7,000 | 2,723 | 542 | 19·9 |
| Guinea | 1954/55 | 2,727 | 1,313 | 37 | 2·8 |
| Ivory Coast | 1961 | 3,340 | 1,416 | 181 | 12·7 |
| Liberia | 1961 | — | 445 | 85 | 19·1 |
| Mali | 1961 | 4,400 | 2,000 | 24 | 1·2 |
| Mauritania | 1962 | — | 356 | 14 | 4·0 |
| Niger | 1960 | 2,610 | 1,371 | 13 | 0·9 |
| Nigeria | 1962 | 40,000 | 17,500 | 1000 | 5·6 |
| Sierra Leone | 1963 | — | 963 | 58 | 6·0 |
| Senegal | 1962 | 3,000 | — | 80 | — |
| Togo | 1961 | 1,500 | 582 | 24 | 4·1 |
| Upper Volta | 1961 | 3,700 | 1,920 | 24 | 1·2 |

The determination of the wages and working conditions of the employed labour force is a matter of considerable importance, even when the numbers involved are relatively insignificant ; as the numbers grow larger it is certainly no exaggeration to say that it becomes a matter of critical significance for the economic and social stability of the country how this function is discharged. Before turning to examine the development of the bargaining institutions, collective procedures and agreements, it is essential to investigate the pattern and structure of employment as it has so far developed.

Accurate and comprehensive information about the distribution of the employed labour force between industries and occupations is unfortunately not readily available for many of the countries. The problem of collecting reliable data is complicated by the difficulties of census taking and such factors as migration, which takes place across frontiers on a considerable scale, and the extent to which many workers are not permanently committed to wage labour. Labour departments of some of the countries have begun the systematic collection of information relating to employment in broad categories and to publish it at regular intervals. In other instances *ad hoc* surveys have been made and estimates arrived at. Unfortunately, however, the industry classifications used are by no means uniform and it is, therefore, necessary to bear these limitations in mind when comparing the distribution of the employed labour force in the countries surveyed.

The distribution of the labour force between the main sectors of employment and the extent to which these sectors are covered by collective agreements will be given later for each country where the information is available. It is in the first instance, however, interesting to compare the distribution of the employed labour force, at the present stage of economic development in the African countries (for which comparable figures are available and reasonably up to date), with the pattern in the European countries in an advanced stage of industrial development.

The striking feature arising out of this comparison is that the high proportion employed in agriculture and the low proportion in manufacturing, in the African countries, is exactly the opposite to the situation in the industrially advanced countries. The proportions employed for wages in agriculture in most of the French-speaking countries, where subsistence farming is a dominant feature, are substantially lower than the figures quoted below ; however, the proportions employed in commerce and construction are frequently greater

3

TABLE 2

PERCENTAGE DISTRIBUTION OF THE EMPLOYED LABOUR FORCE [1]

| Year and Country | Agri-culture | Mining | Manu-facturing | Construc-tion | Elec. + Water | Commerce | Transport | Services | Other |
|---|---|---|---|---|---|---|---|---|---|
| 1961 Kenya | 42·8 | 0·6 | 7·2 | 4·9 | 0·4 | 6·3 | 7·5 | 29·3 | — |
| 1961 S. Rhodesia | 32·8 | 6·7 | 13·6 | 6·2 | 1·0 | 8·4 | 3·8 | 25·8 | 0·2 |
| 1960 Tanganyika | 49·8 | 3·0 | 4·7 | 2·5 | 0·5 | 3·7 | 1·7 | 26·7 | 7·4 |
| 1961 W. Germany | 2·8 | 3·5 | 44·0 | 10·6 | 0·9 | 14·2 | 6·2 | 17·8 | — |
| 1962 U.K.* | 3·9 | 3·0 | 37·0 | 6·8 | 1·6 | 35·4 | 7·0 | 5·3 | — |
| 1961 Norway | 4·9 | 0·8 | 32·8 | 9·7 | 1·2 | 15·9 | 13·2 | 21·5 | — |

* It is apparent that the sharp differences in the numbers employed in commerce and services in the United Kingdom, Western Germany and Norway arise mainly from differences in definitions.

[1] Quoted from *Review of the Economy of Southern Rhodesia 1963.*

4

than is the case in Kenya, Rhodesia and Tanzania.

The small enterprise is common in African countries, not only in agriculture but also in commerce, building and industry ; this type of enterprise is especially concerned with the manufacture of craft products and with many kinds of repair and upkeep required by the community. The small producer sector of economic activity employs in total a substantial number, but most of the employees are members of the enterprise proprietors' family or near relatives.

A main source of employment in all countries is the State. However, there are considerable variations in the percentage of wage earners employed both directly by the Government and in the public services. As will be seen from the following Table the percentage ranges from a high figure of 73 in Mali, to the much lower figures in Chad, Guinea, Kenya and Tanzania. These figures indicate that the private sector has generally reached a level of development where it is responsible for the bulk of the employment in most of the countries. The present proportions could, of course, be greatly altered by a change in policy in any of the countries concerned. However, as most of the countries are anxious to attract foreign investment it is likely that the private sector will continue to remain a significant source of employment in the future. In the past, the principal concentrations of employment outside the public sector have been in plantations, mining, commerce and the services. Manufacturing has been on a small scale, but it is of considerable importance as a source of employment in Rhodesia and is likely to increase gradually in all of the countries.

## SKILLED WORKERS

In the older industrial countries collective bargaining was developed in the first instance by the unions of skilled workers who were intent on advancing and protecting their vocational interests. In the countries of Africa skill has not become associated with organisation ; workers have not organised upon the basis of their skill and no clearly defined cohesive class of skilled workers has appeared. There are several reasons why distinctive groups of skilled workers have not emerged. One of the most important is the absence of formal entry qualifications. African workers have usually been selected for jobs demanding a higher level of skill in their exercise on the basis of their ability to learn on the job or their aptitude displayed in the course of

5

in-plant training schemes. In the absence of formal entry qualifications there is no specific gate through which the unskilled worker must go to qualify, and there is no simple device at hand which can be used to regulate entry into skilled grades.

TABLE 3

ROUGH ESTIMATES OF THE SHARE OF THE PUBLIC SECTOR IN WAGE-EARNING EMPLOYMENT IN SELECTED AFRICAN COUNTRIES [1]

| Country | Year | Estimated Employment in the Public Sector | |
| | | Thousands | Per cent of Total Wage Employment |
| --- | --- | --- | --- |
| I. *Rough but comprehensive estimates* * | | | |
| Chad † | 1961 | 10 | 28 |
| Dahomey ‡ | 1961 | 16 | 44 |
| Ghana | 1960 | 190 | 35 |
| Guinea | 1954–55 | 9 | 24 |
| Kenya | 1960 | 161 | 26 |
| Mali | 1961 | 14 | 73 |
| Mauritania | 1963 | 6 | 43 |
| Nigeria § | 1960 | 307 | 34 |
| Tanzania | 1962 | 101 | 26 |
| Uganda | 1963 | 89 | 40 |
| | | | |
| II. *Rough estimates in Public Services* ‖ | | | |
| Ivory Coast ¶ | 1961 | 28 | 15 |
| Liberia | 1961 | 12 | 14 |
| Libya ** | 1954 | 15 | 12 |
| Malagasy Republic †† | 1961 | 33 | 18 |

\* Include, in principle, all public activities, irrespective of branches of activity. Exceptions are given in footnotes below, so far as information was available.
† Transport and communication probably not included.
‡ Public works not included.
§ Estimated number of wage earners in federal, regional and local government, and public corporations. Data is based on returns from establishments employing ten or more workers.
‖ Include in principle, central, provincial and local government administrations, and public institutions in education and health. Public institutions under transport and communications are, in principle, not included.
¶ Coverage unknown.
** Including post and telegraph.
†† Coverage limited to workers subject to the Labour Code.
[1] This table is quoted from K. C. Doctor and Hans Gallis, *op. cit.*

This situation is closely analogous to that described by Professor Turner in his study of the evolution of the cotton unions in Great Britain.[1] It is Professor Turner's contention that many 'skills' are actually the product of trade unionism itself. African experience provides support for the view that the sharp distinction between skilled and unskilled is not so much the product of technology and strategic position as the institutional device of apprenticeship. In the absence of formal distinctions it is difficult to classify skills and to estimate their significance in supply and demand terms.

In the French-speaking territories, union organisation has followed broadly the pattern of the former metropolitan country, namely, ideological general movements. In the English-speaking countries the pattern of union organisation has been somewhat more complex ; but while skill has played relatively little part, occupation has led to the creation of separate unions, especially in the case of clerical and civil service employees. Since the skill and occupational structure of the labour force has not greatly influenced the pattern of union organisation, neither has it influenced the institutional pattern of collective bargaining. There have been very few examples of unions seeking to negotiate conditions of employment for a specific group of skilled workers with the deliberate design of excluding others from participating. Entry into jobs and unions has been open except where racial differences have been involved.

## RACIAL COMPOSITION

The racial composition of the labour force in certain countries, in particular in the English-speaking countries of East and Central Africa, has had a marked impact on the organisational structure of the trade unions and the pattern of collective bargaining. This was specially the case in the copper-mining industry of Northern Rhodesia, where for many years skilled white miners sought to exploit and preserve their position by the exclusion of non-white unskilled workers from entry into their union and thus from a wide range of more skilled and more highly paid jobs. The behaviour pattern of the white miner of Northern Rhodesia was in the classic tradition of exclusiveness practised by trade union groups in many countries. The peculiar monopolistic strength of their union lay in the combination of racial differences with job demarcation lines. Had the labour

[1] H. A. Turner, *Trade Union Growth, Structures and Policy: A Comparative Study of the Cotton Unions*, George Allen & Unwin, London, 1962.

force been racially homogeneous from the beginning it is possible that there would have been no separate union catering for skilled grades and no restriction on entry into these grades. Railway workers in East Africa, for example, did not divide themselves into separate categories of union according to the skills required on the railroads, as did their counterparts in the U.S.A. and in Great Britain ; with the exception of Asiatic employees, who formed a separate organisation, they were satisfied with one union.

The most significant aspect of the racial situation in most of the African countries, in terms of the development of collective bargaining, is the fact that the largest employers are usually European. In most of the countries, Europeans constitute only a tiny minority of the population, but their role as colonial administrators and as the senior managers of the more important public and private enterprises has inevitably placed them in a position of immense strategic significance. Europeans have also filled jobs in banking, commerce, industry and the public services requiring skills and experience that were not, until comparatively recently, available among indigenous Africans. During the past decade much has changed in this respect and with few exceptions, notably in Zambia and Rhodesia, there are no substantial numbers of Europeans working at intermediate levels.

In 1963, there were a number of agreements that covered solely African, European or Indian workers. These agreements had either been negotiated by a union that confined itself to only one of these racial groups, or else the application of the agreement was restricted to a given category of salaried employees (defined by reference not to race, but to their minimum and maximum pay) recruited, however, up to this stage exclusively from a single ethnic group. This situation is withering away as the racial criterion of employment disappears and Africanisation takes place. With this development the vestiges of racial exclusiveness to be found in union organisation are also evaporating.

## THE COVERAGE OF COLLECTIVE AGREEMENTS

The extent to which employees are covered by collective agreements differs widely between sectors and between countries. In the French-speaking countries, where industry-wide agreements exist, they cover more or less all of those who work in the given sectors of the economy. The problem of assessing the number covered by collective agreements is, however, much more difficult in the English-speaking countries of Africa, where the majority of agreements are negotiated upon an enterprise basis. For these various reasons, it is not possible to state precisely the proportion of wage earners that is covered by collective agreements. It may, however, be stated with confidence that the proportion has gone up considerably over the past decade. This increase in the coverage of collective agreements has been due both to the spread of collective bargaining during this period and to the increase in numbers employed. During the past five years the increase in the number of negotiated agreements has been a more important factor than the growth of the employed labour force which in a number of countries may in fact have slightly gone down.

Without at this stage examining what is the difference in the meaning of the agreements, it is possible to give an approximate assessment of coverage in the French- and English-speaking countries.

## In the French-speaking Countries

The system of collective agreements was first introduced into French West Africa in 1937 ; it was extended to Cameroon in 1944, to Madagascar in 1947 and French Equatorial Africa in 1951. During the first period of this development, that is up to the introduction of the 'Labour Code for Overseas Territories' in 1952, there were a few agreements covering the whole Federation of French West Africa which were applicable only to European workers. The African workers on their side were covered by separate agreements made in each territory. This system of federal and territorial agreements was further supplemented by local and regional agreements.

In the following years considerable changes in the status of agreements took place with a marked trend towards centralisation. Without the old agreements being formally denounced, new agreements covering all workers in a particular branch of economic activity, regardless of race or category, were concluded at the federal level, especially from 1956 onwards. As a consequence all the previous ones lost much of their importance ; some of the more recently concluded regional and local agreements were maintained only in the form of an annex to the federal agreement.[1] The salary scales supplementing the federal agreements, however, continued after 1956 to be

[1] For example, the agreement concerning the river transport of Casamance (1955) became an annex to the general agreement for commerce.

9

established, as a rule, within the limits of the territory. By the end of the 1950's the federation of French West Africa was covered by a comprehensive network of federal agreements.[1] In French Equatorial Africa the trend towards federal agreements was not quite as clearly marked as in the case of its neighbour.

This complex of federal, territorial and local agreements, along with a body of labour law, was inherited by the territories when they became independent countries. Some changes have been made, but the legal framework and a whole set of agreements are still in force today. In the countries in which a new labour code has been introduced, such as Senegal and Mali, it states that former agreements will remain in force in so far as they are not contrary to the new code and if other new agreements have not been made. Some of the countries have made, or are in the process of making, revisions in the agreements and others contemplate making changes as the need arises.

With this introduction we are now in a position to outline briefly the broad coverage of collective agreements in each of the countries surveyed. It is, however, necessary to stress that the figures given below are subject to serious reservations as to their reliability. They should be regarded as indicating only the approximate size of the employment groups covered.[2]

*Senegal.* With the number of wage and salary earners estimated in 1962 at 80,000, out of a total population of approximately three million, the most important groups of employees were to be found in the public services, 21,000; commerce, 18,000; manufacturing, 12,000; building, 11,000; transport, 9000; agriculture, 3000; electricity and water services, 2000.[3]

Most of the collective agreements in existence have their origin in the previous Federation of French West Africa, and in the ex-Federation of Mali, which existed from 1959 to 1960. In addition to the federal and territorial agreements, a number of local agreements, concerning in particular workers in bakeries and cinemas, were also made before the State of Senegal took its present form in August 1960. Since that date new agreements covering printing (September 1960), catering (*id.*) and clothing workers (1963) have been concluded. Almost all the agreements have been extended by decree to

---

[1] These covered building and public works (1956); commerce (1956); mechanical industries (1957); transport (1957); textile industries (1958); banks (1958); oil industry (1958); chemical industries (1958); food industries (1958).
[2] The limitations of the data on wage earners in African countries are discussed at greater length by K. C. Doctor and Hans Gallis, *op. cit.*
[3] Source: *Rapport annuel, 1961*, Ministère du Travail et de la Fonction Publique.

all enterprises in the branches of industry covered. The only employed workers not to be covered by collective agreements at the present time are domestic servants and rural workers.

*Ivory Coast.* The statistical information available for this country is more comprehensive than is the case for most of the other French-speaking countries. Recent estimates indicate that the employed wage earners reached in 1962 over 180,000 out of a population of 3,340,000, one of the highest figures in absolute and in percentage terms for this group of countries. The great majority of those workers are covered by collective agreements, concluded in most cases before 1960. According to official estimates, agreements covered some 21,000 employees in construction ; 16,000 in manufacturing industries ; 12,000 in commerce ; 14,000 in transport ; 2000 in mining ; 2600 in catering ; 1600 in electricity and water ; 400 in printing. Not covered by agreements are the 21,000 civil servants, 31,000 agricultural, forestry workers, 3500 seafarers ; domestic servants are also not covered by agreements. The working conditions of these categories of employees are regulated by special decrees.[1]

The desire for a collective agreement has been manifested by the agricultural workers on many occasions, but the establishment of a collective agreement has met with difficulties arising from the fact that a large part of the rural labour is employed seasonally and is composed of migrants. A good many of the migrants come from the Upper Volta and their conditions are regulated by special conventions between the governments of the Ivory Coast and Upper Volta. Another obstacle to the concluding of a collective agreement for the rural workers has stemmed from the opposition of the employers who have feared that any increase in their obligations to their employees would not be compatible with reasonable profit margins and stable prices for agricultural products.

*Dahomey, Niger, Upper Volta and Togo.* The bulk of the economically active population of these countries are engaged in small family-type agricultural enterprises. The number of employed workers represent a very small fraction of the total population : less than 40,000 in Dahomey out of 1,800,000 inhabitants, less than 25,000 in Upper Volta and Togo.[2] In Niger, the proportion of the labour force employed was less than 1 per cent. In each of these countries the collective agreements made during the period of the Federation of

[1] Information supplied by the Ministère du Travail, Côte d'Ivoire.
[2] Source : *Statistiques sur la main-d'œuvre en Haute-Volta.*

French West Africa have remained in force,[1] at least theoretically. Due, however, to the limited economic development, their field of application has not extended much beyond the building industry, commerce, transport and a few services. There have been practically no new developments in collective agreements in these countries since independence, apart from one new agreement concluded in 1963 covering private teachers employed in the Upper Volta. Such improvements in working conditions that have occurred during the past few years have been introduced by employers on their own initiative. In the absence of any significant new economic development leading to the employment of substantial numbers of workers, there has been little opportunity to extend the system of collective agreements. Furthermore, the governments have taken steps to regulate the conditions of employment of those workers not covered by collective agreements by ordinance. For example, in Upper Volta, an ordinance was adopted in February 1960 covering the general conditions of employment of workers not covered by collective agreements.

*Mali.* The total number of wage and salary earners in 1962, according to official statistics, was 24,265, that is, less than 0·5 per cent of the population. Apart from civil servants the main groups of employed are to be found in transport, 2300 ; building, 1800 ; manufacturing industry, 800 ; commerce, 3200 ; and agriculture ('Office du Niger'), 2000.[2]

The agreements made at the time of the Federation remained in force, until they were recently superseded by the adoption of the new labour code. They had also become outdated by the necessity to make wage increases as a result of a rise in the cost of living. Since Mali became independent, considerable changes have taken place in the structure and organisation of the economy. The private sector has been gradually reduced in size ; what remains has been brought under public control. Industrial relations are now in fact dominated by the Government, which is undertaking a general review of the provisions of the existing agreements. In accordance with the policy of the Government, which is to reduce the differences in the conditions of employment of various categories of workers, the intention is to reduce the number of agreements to six and to broaden the application of each — for example, one agreement will cover all employment in industry.

---

[1] They were applied in Togo before independence although that territory was never part of the former Federation.  [2] Source : Ministère du Travail.

*Guinea.* In Guinea, with 37,000 wage earners, out of a labour force of 1·3 million, the developments taking place are similar to those observed in Mali. The old agreements, still unchanged at the end of 1963, were to be replaced by new ones in course of preparation. During the past few years improvements in working conditions have been granted by employers unilaterally with the tacit acceptance of the Government. The formal adoption of new conditions — whether taking the form of agreements or of administrative regulation — is a matter of government initiative. When the process of revision is completed this is likely to mean that workers in practically all industries will come within the scope of an agreement ; the number of agreements will be reduced while the field of application of each will be extended.

*Mauritania.* In 1962 a general collective agreement was made which replaced all previous agreements. The new agreement covers building, manufacturing industries, transport, mining, commerce and food. Special annexes to the agreement make provision for the specific needs of workers in these different industries. Further supplementary provisions are being prepared to cover fishermen and domestic servants. Thus, all of the 14,300 wage earners will soon be covered, except in agriculture where there is little employed labour. Outside the building industry with 6800 employees and mining with 2300, the groups covered are all very small and do not exceed a few hundred people.[1]

The establishment of a single agreement covering all workers is the final stage of evolution towards the standardisation of conditions of employment which can be observed in a number of the French-speaking countries and which sooner or later is likely to be adopted by several of them.

*Central African Republic.* In 1961, it was estimated that the total number of wage and salary earners employed in the Central African Republic was approximately 48,000, out of a total population rather greater than 1,100,000.[2] Some twenty collective agreements are in force at the time of writing. Certain of these have been inherited from the former Federation of Equatorial Africa and they cover manufacturing industry, commerce and banks. Other agreements were made within the framework of the former territory, then of the autonomous Republic, of Oubangui-Chari. After independence three new agreements were made covering the catering industry, the Shell

[1] Source : Ministère de la Santé du Travail des Affaires Sociales et de la Fonction Publique.  [2] See Table 1.

13

Company and the cotton industry. The agreements at present in force, which do not cover more than one-half of the 48,000 employees, include manufacturing industries, 4200 ; commerce, 3800 ; transport, 2000 ; certain public services such as the office of Social Benefits and Post and Telegraphs, 6000. Not covered by agreements are 10,000 workers in agriculture, 8000 in forestry and 3000 in mining.

*Chad.* Out of a population of 2,600,000 in 1961 42,000 were employed wage earners. Of this number 8500 were in industry, 3500 in building, 7000 in commerce, 15,000 in government services and 5000 were employed as domestic servants.[1] Relatively little development of the system of collective agreements has taken place in recent years ; the old ones have not been revised and few new agreements have been negotiated after independence ; an exception to this general situation was the adoption, in 1962, of a new agreement covering building and public works in place of an earlier one made in 1955. Little use has been made of the procedure of extension, widely resorted to in the other French-speaking countries, the only example being the agreement covering commerce. The limited development of collective agreements in Chad is attributed to unfavourable economic and social conditions and to a projected reform of the labour code which has inhibited the negotiation of new agreements.

*Congo (Brazzaville).* The total number employed in Congo-Brazzaville in 1960 was probably rather less than 50,000. Of this number some 9000 were employed in agriculture, 2300 in mining and quarrying, 5500 in manufacture, 4300 in construction, 8000 in commerce, 5000 in transport, 750 in public utilities and 11,000 in various service occupations.[2] Although the employed population is small, most of it is covered by collective agreements, the principal groups excluded being agricultural workers and domestic servants. Among the numerous agreements which are in force (22) many have been concluded since 1960, and most others have been revised in 1962 and 1963.

*Gabon.* Out of a total population of approximately 500,000 some 44,000 are employed for wages and salaries, the largest number being employed in agriculture, forestry and fishing, 13,000 ; mining, 6500 ; manufacturing, 4000 ; building, 3700 ; transport, 2600 ; commerce, 5500 ; and services, 6500.[3] There are no data available

[1] Source : *International Labour Review*, May 1962, and Table 1.
[2] See *International Labour Review*, December 1961 and Table 1.
[3] Source : *ILO Statistical Return, 1963.*

on the recent development of collective negotiations in that country, where the federal agreements of the former AEF seem to be still in force.

*Cameroon.* Almost one-half of the 100,000 employed for wages and salaries in 1960 (43,000) were employed in agriculture, especially on the plantations ; 10,000 in mining and manufacture ; 6000 in construction ; 6000 in transport and communications ; 21,000 in commerce ; and 19,000 in various services.[1] Between 1955 and 1959 eleven collective agreements were concluded. They all remain in force today, except the agreement covering banana plantations which was revoked in 1962. Two new agreements were made in 1962 and 1963 ; the first covered road transport ; the second covered workers employed in forestry. Where the agreement has covered only a particular enterprise, following practice in the former metropolitan country, it has been extended by decree to cover all other workers in the same branch of industry. The conditions of employment laid down in the agreement covering building and public works was made applicable to all workers employed by the Government other than established civil servants. Thus the great majority of the 100,000 wage-earners in the country were covered except 6000 domestic workers whose condition of employment is regulated by an ordinance passed in 1956, agricultural workers other than those employed in forestry, and civil servants.

*Malagasy Republic.* Out of a total of 206,000 gainfully employed in 1960, the largest numbers were to be found in the public services, 48,000 ; agriculture, forestry and fishing, 45,000 ; domestic service, 32,000 ; commerce, 26,000 ; manufacturing industry, 18,000 ; transport, 15,000 ; building, 10,000 ; and mining, 7000.[2]

Before independence only the employees in banks and those in the sugar industry were covered by collective agreements ; however, since 1961 several new agreements have been concluded. These cover workers in the electrical power industry, railway employers, dockers at the port of Tamatave and members of the Institute of Scientific Research of the Malagasy Republic. The biggest group of wage earners whose conditions of employment are regulated by a collective agreement is that employed on the sugar plantations, numbering 8000, about one-fifth of all wage earners in agriculture. However, the number all-told covered by collective agreements is

---

[1] Source : *Rapport au gouvernement de la République fédérale du Cameroun sur une mission inter-organisation d'enquête sur la main-d'œuvre*, ILO 1962.

[2] *Rapport du gouvernement de la République Malgache sur l'emploi et la formation professionnelle*, 1963.

still rather small, some 13,000 out of the total for all employees given above.

### In the English-speaking Countries

Turning now to the former British territories of West, East and Central Africa, we find a greater diversity of development than in the former French territories. It is doubtful if there were any collective agreements in existence in the former British territories before 1938, other than in the Northern Rhodesian copper-mining industry where the white miners had formed a union in 1936 and commenced collective bargaining. In most of the other countries collective bargaining began during and after the Second World War.[1] Labour departments actively encouraged employers to recognise unions and to enter into procedural agreements for the purpose of regulating the negotiation of voluntary collective agreements. The development of collective bargaining spread rapidly during the 1950's so that by the early 1960's a substantial proportion of employees in most English-speaking territories was covered by a collective agreement of some kind. Most of these agreements cover a single enterprise and there are relatively few industry-wide agreements negotiated at the national level. Another rather sharp difference in the situation between the two groups of countries is that in the English-speaking ones employees in plantations are quite well organised and often covered by collective agreements; this is hardly ever the case in the French-speaking countries.

*Zambia.* The total number of employed workers in 1961 was 269,000. Of this number the largest element was employed in the services, 92,000; building, 32,000; mining and quarrying, 51,000; agriculture, 37,000; manufacturing, 20,000; commerce, 22,000; transport and communications, 13,000; and electricity, gas and water, 3000.[2]

The most important collective agreements are undoubtedly those that cover the 40,000 employees in the copper mines. There have been separate agreements covering the 33,000 African mineworkers; the 4000 specialised highly skilled workers — mainly European; the European staff; the African supervisors and clerical employees; and the mines' 'policemen'. The trend is, however, in the direction of eliminating all distinctions based upon racial differences, leaving

---

[1] The early developments are examined by B. C. Roberts, *Labour in the Tropical Territories of the Commonwealth:* G. Bell, London, 1964.
[2] *Annual Report of the Labour Department,* 1963.

only those arising out of manifestly different job categories.

Most of the 8000 workers in transport, 1500 in the food industry and 400 in printing appear to be covered by agreements as well as a considerable proportion of the workers employed by the Government. The workers in the construction industry and in motor repair and trading are covered by agreements concluded within the framework of Joint Industrial Councils which are given the force of law by statutory orders.

In other branches of employment where trade union organisation has not yet reached the stage where it has been able to negotiate agreements, wage councils have been constituted on the initiative of the Government. These bodies, which ensure the participation of union representatives, employers and independent persons, have the statutory authority to determine minimum wages and certain conditions of employment that are legally binding upon employers. They cover among others the retail trade, African employees in the building industry, hotels and restaurants. The minimum wages of Africans, except domestic servants, who are not covered by a collective agreement or a wages council, are determined by an independent wages board whose recommendations serve as a basis for statutory orders.

*Kenya.* In this country, the total number of workers employed for a wage or salary reached in 1961, 620,000 out of a total population of 7,000,000. Of this number 90 per cent were African, 6 per cent Asian and 4 per cent European. The main sectors of employment are agriculture, forestry and fishing, 245,000 ; national and local government and public services, 168,000 ; domestic and other services, 45,000 ; manufacturing, 45,000 ; commerce, 43,000 ; building, 13,000 ; transport and communications, 16,000 ; mining, 3500 ; electricity, water and sanitary services, 2500.[1]

Collective agreements are numerous — they are numbered by hundreds — and cover high proportions — 60 to 100 per cent — of workers employed in all sectors of economic activity. Eighty per cent of the workers employed in the most important sector of employment in Kenya — namely agriculture — are covered by collective agreements. The conditions of employment in each special branch of agriculture, sisal, coffee, tea, 'mixed farming', are governed by a single agreement. The majority of agreements in other sectors have been negotiated at the enterprise level. In spite of the high degree of general coverage, as might be expected from universal

[1] *Annual Report, Labour Department,* 1962.

experience, many small employers have been able to ignore collective bargaining. In those sectors where union organisation is generally difficult because of the small-scale units of employment and the dispersion of the workers, such as garment making, laundries, building, road transport, garages and bakeries, statutory minimum wages are established by wages boards. Area minima have been fixed for all workers employed in Nairobi and Mombasa as well as in some other towns of lesser importance. The main groups of workers, whose conditions of employment remain outside all forms of regulation, are to be found among the agricultural workers employed outside the plantations and large farms, to whom existing agreements do not extend and who are not subject to the statutory minimum; the fixing of a minimum wage rate for the whole of agricultural employment is under consideration in Kenya.

*Uganda.* Out of a total population of 6,500,000 it is officially estimated that some 350,000 workers are employed for wages and salaries. Of this number over 135,000 are employed in agriculture (about 85,000 on small farms). Some 67,000 in central and local government service; 28,000 in building and construction; 25,000 in hotels, restaurants and domestic services; 10,000 in commerce; 10,000 in transport and communications; 8000 in food and drink; 5000 in mines and cement; 2500 in textiles; printing, 1500.[1]

Collective agreements have been signed covering approximately 25 per cent of the workers employed in agriculture; 90 per cent of those employed in transport and communications, mines and cement, tobacco manufacture; 50 to 60 per cent of those employed in textiles and printing; and 20 to 30 per cent of those employed in hotels, restaurants, commerce, building and construction. A number of agreements also exist for employees in central and local administration. Collective bargaining, however, is still in a very early stage of development in Uganda and many of the agreements signed up to 1953 were to do with recognition and procedure. Bargaining on actual wages and other working conditions has not yet developed far in a number of sectors of employment. However, workers not covered by collective agreements have the protection of wages boards with power to establish legal minimum rates of pay.

*Tanzania.* Out of a total population of 9,100,000 some 390,000 were employed for wages and salaries in 1962. The largest group of employees is to be found in agriculture, 197,000, of which 130,000 are employed in the sisal plantations. The other principal employ-

[1] Source: Department of Labour.

18

ment sectors are national and local government services, 65,000 ; building and construction, 41,000 ; manufacturing industry, 28,000 ; transport and communications, 23,000 ; commerce, 17,000 ; mining, 9000 ; electricity, water and sanitary services, 5000.[1]

Collective agreements had already become an important feature of the system of industrial relations in Tanzania, when, in 1962, compulsory arbitration was introduced. Since then wages and working conditions have been in most cases the subject of awards. In agriculture, for example, the wages of the sisal workers were fixed by an award in 1962. Nevertheless independent negotiations were carried on regarding the right and duties of union representatives and the employers and an agreement was signed in August 1963. In 1965 the Sisal Growers' Association concluded with the National Union of Workers a comprehensive new agreement on wages and a new procedural agreement. In other branches of agriculture, tea plantations for example, wages have been settled by free negotiation. It has been estimated that some 85 per cent of all agricultural workers are covered by an agreement of one kind or another. The proportion is similar in the food industry, which employs some 8000 workers ; it is surprisingly still higher in building and public works, which is one of the largest sectors of employment. Transport, mines, manufacturing and the distribution of petroleum products are all practically completely covered by agreements. The coverage is rather lower in commerce, wood products and garment making. Most of the agreements outside agriculture are concluded at the enterprise level.

Most of the workers who are not covered by an agreement have the protection of minimum wage legislation.

*Rhodesia (Southern).* Out of a total population of approximately four million in 1962, just over 220,000 were of European origin. The total number of employees of all races was 700,000. Apart from agriculture, 239,000, the largest number of paid workers were in the manufacturing industry, 95,000, and domestic service, 95,000 ; some 86,000 were employed in public administration, education, health and other types of services ; of the 59,000 employees in commerce and finance, 23,000 were of European or Asiatic origin ; the mining industry employed 47,000 ; construction, 44,000 ; transport and communications, 27,000 ; and electricity and water supply, 7000.

[1] Source : *Report on Employment and Earnings in Tanganyika* (February 1963), prepared by the Statistics Division of the Treasury.

# Collective Bargaining in African Countries

A substantial proportion of the total number of employees are covered by collective agreements. Separate agreements have been negotiated in the mines for mineworkers and for the clerical and supervisory staff. These agreements cover about 85 per cent of the total personnel employed in the mines. The proportion of employees covered by collective agreements is similar in the manufacturing and textile industries and among workers employed in transport and public administration. On the other hand not more than 35 per cent of the wage earners employed in commerce in the urban areas are covered by agreements. Printing is also covered to approximately the same extent, which is perhaps a little surprising since this industry is usually highly organised and most of its employees are covered by agreements. Employees in metal works are covered to a lesser extent (25 per cent), while the percentage in construction is still lower (10 per cent). So far in construction and also in the chemical industry only the higher paid workers have the benefit of collective agreements.

*Malawi.* Out of a population of approximately 3 million, 140,000 were recorded as employed wage earners in 1961. Of this number the largest group of workers was employed in national and local government and other services 40,000; on the plantations, 34,000; tobacco handling, 7000 ; railways, 5000 ; commerce, 12,000 ; building and construction, 3500.[1]

In May 1964 eleven collective agreements were apparently in force covering some 51,000 wage earners. Eight of these agreements were procedural agreements entered into for the purpose of establishing joint industrial councils through which wages and working conditions could be fixed. However, the agreements covering plantations, railways and the distribution of petroleum products were of a comprehensive kind covering wages scales or other conditions of employment.

*Ghana.* The employed labour force constitutes a relatively high proportion of the whole population, more than 500,000 out of approximately 7,000,000. More than a quarter of this number in 1960 was employed in agriculture, 152,000 ; in the public services some 117,000. The other half of the working population is divided into five groups of fairly comparable size, building and construction, 65,000 ; commerce, 42,000 ; transport and communications, 40,000 ; mining and quarrying, 39,000 ; manufacturing, 23,000.[2]

[1] Report from Department of Labour, Nyasaland.
[2] Statistical Return — ILO, 1960.

20

## The Areas of Employment covered by Collective Agreements

Collective bargaining is widely developed and numerous agreements exist covering a substantial proportion of employees. In the majority of cases the agreements cover only a single enterprise and often only a particular group of employees. However, there are industry-wide agreements covering plantations, gold and bauxite mines, civil engineering and wood products. In other cases, for example banks and the distribution of petroleum products, the agreements though concluded on an enterprise basis cover a wide proportion of that sector of employment.

*Nigeria.* The largest country in Africa in terms of population with the total employed for wages and salaries perhaps one million. Official figures relate to a much smaller number, some 473,000, in 1959. Of this number the largest groups employed were to be found in national and local government and public services, 160,000; building and construction, 103,000; transport and communications, 48,000; agriculture, forestry and fishing, 46,000; commerce, 42,000; mining and quarrying, 41,000; manufacturing, 32,000.[1]

There are a good many collective agreements in Nigeria, mainly negotiated on an enterprise basis. The most important one concerns the coal mining industry for which agreements have existed for quite a number of years. Other agreements cover substantial numbers of workers employed on plantations (8000), in the oil producing and petroleum distribution industry (3000), railways (24,000), ports (10,000), manufacturing, building and commerce.

It is impossible to say with any degree of precision what proportion of the employed labour force is covered by collective agreements, partly because of the diffuse character of the Nigerian trade union movement, the regional structure of the country and lack of reliable employment statistics.

*Sierra Leone.* It was estimated in 1961 that some 52,000 persons were employed in establishments with more than six employees. Small establishments, it was thought, might account for another 35,000 to 50,000 employees. The largest group of employees in 1961 were in government administration and public services, 27,000; in the private sector mining, 6100; building and construction, 11,000; commerce, 5000; agriculture, forestry and fishing, 2500[2]; manufacturing, 3600; and transport and communications, 9000.

Over the past twenty years a comprehensive system of joint industrial councils and wages boards has been established through which

[1] Source: *International Labour Review*, December 1961.
[2] Source: *Annual Report of Labour Department*, 1960.

the terms and conditions of employment are determined by trade union representatives and employers. Five or six collective agreements have been negotiated in commerce covering approximately 2500 workers, employed in the Bank of West Africa and several commercial firms.

*Gambia.* One of the smallest countries in Africa, Gambia had a employed labour force of 9643 in December 1962. The largest group of employees, 5198, were employed by the central government in administrative and other services ; commercial and other private establishments employed 3655 persons; local government, 483 ; and a public corporation 307.

Following industrial unrest, joint industrial councils were established in 1960, for wage earners in (1) the building and civil engineering industry ; (2) road transport and mechanical engineering ; (3) commerce (including wholesale and retail trade, hotel and catering services) ; (4) port industry (docks and river transport) ; (5) agriculture. Each of these groups has since been covered by collective agreements negotiated through the joint industrial councils.

In addition to the joint industrial councils the senior civil servants are covered by a National Whitley Council and discussions are taking place with a view to establishing other Whitley Councils for junior grades in the civil service and teachers.

*Liberia.* Approximately 20 per cent of the labour force is employed for wages and salaries, but it seems that so far few collective agreements have been negotiated. However dockers, seafarers and miners are covered by agreements. Since the country is in principle in favour of collective bargaining the relatively slow progress of this method of regulating the conditions of employment may be attributed to the comparatively low level of economic development and the weak state of the trade union movement. However, there are signs that some of the foreign firms who have hitherto not engaged in collective bargaining, now feel that it would be wise to enter into agreements on the matter of wages and the working conditions of their employees and several agreements were under discussion in 1964.

Apart from the two main groups of countries which have been examined in the previous pages, there is a certain number of countries which have to be considered separately, for one thing because they never came under British or French influence — at least not to the same extent — and secondly because collective negotiations have not started yet or have not known any significant development.

## The Areas of Employment covered by Collective Agreements

In the *Sudan* restrictions imposed on union activity in 1958, together with the low level of economic development, have not encouraged the development of collective agreements. However, in 1962 the Shell Oil Company entered into an agreement covering its employees engaged in the distribution of petroleum products. At the end of 1963 negotiations were taking place concerning employees in several important enterprises including a cement works, a brewery and a hardware factory ; in addition negotiations were taking place concerning the employment of some 10,000 wage earners employed driving and repairing vehicles used in the administration of the 'Gezira Scheme'. Joint consultation was also said to take place in the smaller enterprises for the settlement of particular problems. There is no statutory minimum wage of any kind in the Sudan and in the absence of collective bargaining, wage rates and conditions are set unilaterally by the employer perhaps after a certain degree of individual bargaining with the worker.

In *Somalia* four agreements have been concluded since 1961 ; two of them concern rural enterprises, another governs working conditions in ports and the most recent covers employees of the petroleum company AGIP. It is unlikely that much further development will take place until a higher level of economic activity is achieved.

In *Ethiopia*, at the end of 1963, trade union organisation was in process — 43 workers' unions had been registered and employers on their part were constituting their own agency — and a model agreement was being prepared at the Ministry of Labour ; but, though they were in principle favoured by the Government, collective negotiations had hardly started. In matters of remuneration, there was no statutory minimum ; wages were being paid according to custom. The only known agreement, signed in 1964, covers the workers of a sugar estate.

In the *Congo (Kinshasa)*, where the total number of employed was reported to be 1,180,000 in 1955 — which was the highest figure for all the countries examined — a new ordinance was passed in October 1963 to serve as a basis for the conclusion of collective agreements ; it has a good deal in common with the legislation existing in the other French-speaking countries. One could hardly expect a rapid development of the system in the critical political context which prevailed since independence. However, a first agreement was concluded in 1965 for Sabena Airlines and others are being negotiated.

Chapter 2

# THE TRADE UNIONS

COLLECTIVE bargaining can begin only when certain conditions
have been fulfilled. One of the most important conditions is that
there should be in existence trade unions which have reached a stage
of development where they are sufficiently strong to persuade employers that it would be to their advantage to agree to settle the terms
and conditions of employment by a negotiated collective agreement ;
or that, if the unions are weak, the State is prepared to promote
collective bargaining artificially by the passing of specific laws which
compel employers to recognise trade unions and to bargain in good
faith. The rights of workers to join unions and of unions to negotiate
with employers were implicitly protected by the Labour Codes which
were adopted in the former French territories. In former British
territories such positive protection was not provided, since it was
believed it would make the unions dependent upon the State to a
degree that might be inimical to their development. However, since
independence several countries, notably Ghana and Tanzania, have
introduced legislation modelled on that which has existed in the
United States since 1935, making it an offence for an employer to
refuse to bargain with a properly accredited trade union.

The ability of unions to bargain effectively and responsibly depends
upon their organisational strength. When unions have few members,
a low income and little funds, employers are generally in a position
to refuse them recognition and to discourage their employees from
joining. Even if compelled by law to recognise unions and to
negotiate with them, employers are able to evade their undertakings
if the unions are weak and unable effectively to police the agreements
that have been signed. The strength of the unions is a vital factor whatever the system of industrial relations, whether this system is closer to
an administrative process in which the State plays a dominant role,
or to one in which the unions depend upon their own power to persuade
employers to enter into collective agreements. In these circumstances
a system of statutory joint Industrial Councils or compulsory arbitration may be an important means of helping the unions to acquire

24

the status and build up the power necessary to bargain effectively. The strength of unions in Africa varies widely. Some are reasonably strong, many are extremely weak, but most of them have reached the stage where they are involved in some form of collective negotiation. The pattern of collective bargaining and the types of agreement reached are closely related to the pattern of union organisation and the legal framework of the industrial relations' system. In this respect there are considerable differences between the former British and former French colonial territories.

## TRADE UNION STRUCTURE AND COLLECTIVE BARGAINING IN ENGLISH-SPEAKING COUNTRIES

The influence of the metropolitan countries on the pattern of union organisation and the pattern of collective bargaining has been considerable. In the former British territories unions were encouraged to grow on the basis of the common interest of a group of employees of a particular employer. Following British experience, political and ideological factors were generally discouraged as an appropriate basis of union organisation. Thus the form of union organisation in the former British territories has reflected the structural characteristics of employment to a far greater extent than has been the case in the former French territories. In the British territories a small number of large unions catering for employees in the Government and public services and such major enterprises as mining, generally developed side by side with a large number of small enterprise unions. This was particularly the case in West Africa, where in 1958 there were no fewer than 268 unions in Nigeria, 69 in Ghana. Sierra Leone, with only 23 unions, was a significant exception in West Africa that illustrates the importance of the relationship between union structure and the pattern of collective bargaining. In Sierra Leone, wages and working conditions are determined through a system of industry-wide joint industrial councils and wages boards instead of through enterprise bargaining. This system of wage determination together with a registration law designed to discourage the growth of many small organisations has kept down the number of unions. In the East and Central African countries the number of unions are much fewer than in Nigeria and they have tended to cover a whole industry or service more often than has been the case in West Africa.[1] The general

[1] In 1958 there were registered in Kenya 42 unions, in Northern Rhodesia 22, Nyasaland 4, Tanganyika 30, Uganda 19, Zanzibar 19.

trend, even in West Africa, would nevertheless appear to be following the same pattern as in the older industrial countries, as urbanisation and industrialisation take place ; namely, towards larger units of organisation. It is interesting to note that while the average trade union in Nigeria had only 750 members, the largest trade unions have between them some 50 per cent of the total trade union membership.[1]

Where unions exist on an industry-wide scale they tend to seek industry-wide agreements, but the achievement of this objective depends upon the structure of the employing organisation. If an entire industry is in the hands of a single employer then an industry-wide agreement and an enterprise agreement become co-terminous. If an industry consists of many employers it is obvious that an industrial union could not of itself bring about an industry-wide agreement — this can only be achieved if the employers are also prepared to associate for the purpose of negotiating a common agreement. There have, in fact, been important developments of employers' organisations in the English-speaking African countries that have had a powerful effect on the structure of collective bargaining and agreements. These developments are discussed in a later chapter.

The trend towards a more concentrated union membership in a compact number of large industry-wide organisations was drastically speeded up in Ghana with the passing of the Industrial Relations Act in 1958, and its subsequent amendments. This legislation reshaped the pattern of union organisation, reducing 158 unions to 16 and giving the Ghana TUC great authority to co-operate and direct the industrial and political policy of the trade unions. The change in the structure of the unions was accompanied by major changes in the industrial relations system. The limitation of bargaining rights to certificated unions and the adoption of a form of compulsory arbitration, gave additional support to centripetal trends already evident. Enterprise bargaining is still important in Ghana, but the course is set towards a greater degree of centralisation in procedures and uniformity in standards ; how far this has proceeded will be discussed in Chapter 4. Another drastic and, in some respects, similar approach to the reshaping of union organisation and the concentration of authority at the top of the movement, has taken place in Tanzania since independence. In this case all trade unions have been made, as it were, constituent elements of one big union. Steps

[1] Roberts, *op. cit.* p. 123.

26

to strengthen the central trade union organisations have also been
taken in Kenya, Zambia and Sierra Leone without going as far as in
Ghana and Tanzania.

## TRADE UNION STRUCTURE AND COLLECTIVE BARGAINING IN THE FRENCH-SPEAKING COUNTRIES

The pattern of union organisation adopted in the former French
territories followed that developed in France. The influence of the
metropolitan country was even greater than in the case of the former
English territories. From 1937 to 1944 the trade union organisations
were in fact an extension of those existing in France. During this
period trade union membership was restricted to a limited number
by literacy requirements, but after these were swept away in 1944,
unions grew rapidly under the aegis of the metropolitan federations.
By the mid-1950's over 130,000 workers belonged to the central
organisations in French West Africa.[1]

The Confédération Générale du Travail, with a total of 47,000
members, was the most important organisation in the Federation of
French West Africa, the Federation of French Equatorial Africa and
the Cameroon. The Confédération des Travailleurs Chrétiens with
a total membership of 49,400, exceeding that of the CGT, was far
and away the most important organisation in Madagascar where its
membership was 33,500 members, but elsewhere it fell behind the
CGT. The third organisation, the Confédération Générale du Travail
— Force Ouvrière, with a total membership of 12,000, mainly white
collar and European workers, was a numerically much less powerful
organisation than the other two bodies. There were in addition to
these three organisations, in Madagascar, a Federation of Local Administrative Workers, and an Autonomous Centre of Administrative
Workers, and in all of the countries there was a significant minority
of independent unions.

The situation began to change when in 1955 the General Confederation of Labour in Senegal and Mauritania decided to establish
an independent organisation, the General Confederation of African
Workers. The developments that followed in those and other areas
of French Africa were infinitely complex, but they finally resulted in
a complete separation from the metropolitan organisations and the

[1] P. F. Gonidec, 'The Development of Trade Unionism in Black Africa', *Bulletin of the Inter-African Labour Institute*, vol. x, no. 2, 1963.

creation of autonomous African trade union centres.[1]  In the event, however, the general pattern of organisation followed by the various countries was similar to that of previous metropolitan trade union organisations.  The ideological attachment of the unions had become primarily to African nationalism, though they were still influenced by the two world organisations of trade unions, the ICFTU and WFTU.

In 1957 the former CGT and an element which had broken away, formed a Union Générale des Travailleurs d'Afrique Noire (UGTAN).  The Federation of Christian Workers dropped the word 'Chrétiens' for 'Croyants' and evolved into the Pan African Confederation of Believing Workers, but with little change in ideological position.  To make the new developments even more closely similar to the previous situation, there also emerged a General Union of Workers of Black Africa, closely linked with the International Confederation of Free Trade Unions.  Thus there emerged three ideologically-based organisations similar in structure and function to their predecessors, differing only in their independence from the former metropolitan unions.

In Mali and Guinea the Marxist-oriented affiliates to UGTAN are today the dominant organisations and they are not prepared to tolerate the existence of any rival body that might threaten this position.  They are sustained by their close relation to the political party in power, and their leaders firmly stress UGTAN's political role.  In Madagascar, and certain other countries, the Confederation of Believing Workers is the principal organisation.  Unlike the UGTAN the Confederation of Believing Workers seeks to keep itself independent of the political authority.  The Confederation rejects both Communism and Capitalism, but is prepared to participate in the 'planning, organisation and control of the economy', in so far as this is desirable to protect the economic interests of the workers. The unions in Senegal and a number of other countries have sought to maintain a precarious independence of the political party in power, but there is a recognition that they cannot afford to come into conflict with the Government.  This desire to see the political success of independence firmly established, together with the clearly manifested determination of all governments not to permit the trade unions to become the centre of an opposition that could undermine their political stability, has led many observers to conclude that union

[1] For a full account of these developments see P. F. Gonidec, *op. cit.*, E. Berg, 'French West Africa' in W. Galenson (ed.), *Labour and Economic Development*, John Wiley, New York, 1959 ; Jean Meynaud and Amine Salah-Bey, *Le Syndicalisme africain*, Paris, 1963.

independence is an illusion. There can be little doubt that in most of the French territories any serious attempt by the unions to oppose the Government's policy would not be tolerated, but this does not mean that the unions are not allowed to develop their economic role within this limitation.

The central federations are composed, as they are in France, of industrial unions organised in local, city and regional units. It is normal policy to group all the unions, irrespective of their specific industrial or occupational interest into a regional federation, which then acts on their behalf as if it were one big union. The local units of organisation are usually extremely weak and there is for the most part no unit of organisation or effective representation at the place of work. In this respect the structure of the union organisation is remarkably similar to that which has long prevailed in much of French industry.

This pattern of union organisation in the French-speaking African countries is closely related to the system of industrial relations that prevails. The essence of the French system is that it seeks to determine the basic conditions of employment, minimum wages, basic hours, holidays and other provisions by a statutory legal code supplemented by collective agreements. The principal function of the unions is to bring such social and political pressure to bear as will bring about a steady improvement in the legal standards laid down. In this respect trade-union action is always and inevitably political action. However, since in addition to the standards of employment laid down nationally there are supplementary industrial and enterprise agreements that enhance the statutory provisions that apply to most workers, the unions also have to exercise negotiating functions directly with employers.

The tactics of the unions as bargaining agents have varied considerably. Prior to the achievement of independence, many strikes occurred, but for the most part these were demonstrations of protest against the administration rather than carefully calculated bargaining pressures designed to induce reluctant employers to conclude a better agreement. It was, of course, difficult, if not impossible, prior to independence to disentangle the desire to protest against European domination from the desire for an immediate improvement in wages and working conditions.

The evolution from this type of demonstration protest to the exerting of bargaining pressures designed to win specific improvements in wages and working conditions, is a vital stage in the development of a collective bargaining system. This step will be taken in a different way when the whole system of industrial relations is predicated upon a legal code and change is, therefore, essentially a political decision, than when issues in dispute between a union and an employer or employers' association have to be resolved without reference to legally imposed standards.

Thus in the French-speaking countries there are relatively few independently negotiated collective agreements. Most collective agreements are made through a mixed labour commission with the assistance of an Inspecteur du Travail. This is not to suggest that the process contains no element of independent collective bargaining, but that the constraints greatly limit the freedom of the parties to develop an independent role. What is more, the bargaining position of the unions at local or enterprise level has been, and still is, extremely weak. Organisation at the place of work is almost non-existent. The pattern has always been that of securing a general agreement that applies to the broadest possible occupational group and the widest geographical coverage. The system of industrial relations and the pattern of collective bargaining in the French-speaking countries of Africa has, in these various respects, followed fairly closely that which prevails in France.

## THE STRENGTH OF THE UNIONS

It is often asserted that the unions in Africa are too weak to bargain effectively. If the ability to bargain is measured in the conventional terms of union membership, financial strength, quality of leadership and administrative efficiency, then it is idle to contest that unions in Africa are much less strong than their counterparts in the more advanced countries.

Union membership has often been unstable. This has been due to three main factors :

(1) A large part of the labour force has been uncommitted to permanent wage employment ; migration has been a major feature of the supply and seasonal employment a characteristic of the demand, especially for agricultural labour.

(2) Acceptance of the notion of belonging to a union as an essential function of employment in the modern sector only becomes a social norm after a lengthy period of time. Many unions have not been in existence long enough for workers to develop a close and continuous attachment. A new generation brought

up to regard unions as a vital social necessity may well not be inhibited by this factor.

(3) Union rivalries, corruption, opportunistic leadership and failure to achieve promised goals, have all contributed to a fluctuating membership.

It must, however, be pointed out that union membership, calculated on the basis of contributions paid at regular intervals, understates the extent of 'membership' if membership is calculated in terms of active support. Many Africans consider themselves to be union members even if they have paid no financial contributions for a long time, and such non-paying members can be relied upon to participate in a demonstration, and even to support a sustained stoppage designed to persuade an employer to concede improved terms. However, a continuous dues-paying attachment to the union is required if its organisational strength is to be built up.

Organisational weakness due to an inadequate flow of funds has to some extent been met by the negotiation of 'check-off' agreements in the English-speaking territories of Africa. Under these agreements the employer undertakes to deduct the appropriate amount of union contribution from the wages of his workers on receipt of a written authorisation from each of them. This method of collecting union contributions appears not to have developed in the French-speaking countries, and in at least one of them, Mali, it would be illegal under Article 306 of the Labour Code.

'Check-off' agreements, while ensuring a steady flow of funds, are sometimes criticised on the score of weakening the bargaining strength of unions by making them dependent upon employers for the collection of union contributions. The willingness of employers to enter into these agreements is occasionally cited as evidence that they stand to benefit in this respect. There is little evidence, however, to suggest that unions have been put under duress by such agreements and compelled to accept terms less favourable than would otherwise have been the case.

In Ghana and Tanzania employers may be compelled by law to deduct union contributions from the pay packets of their employees. In this case there can be no danger that an employer might threaten to refuse to collect the dues unless the union adjusts its behaviour to his demands.

There are, however, more subtle dangers in the use of the 'check-off' that must be considered. When a union is able to rely upon the employer to collect the contributions of its members it is under no pressure to build up a system of voluntary local leaders that will provide the organisational links between the members and the paid union officers at the highest level. In other words the 'check-off' tends to promote a bureaucratic form of organisation and to weaken the grass-roots vitality of the union. It may be argued, however, against this view that the over-all efficiency of the organisation, especially in terms of the ability to employ expert officials, exceeds the loss in other respects. The gain from the point of view of collective bargaining may be particularly significant, since the professional trade union official, who is reasonably well paid and enjoys financial security, is generally more capable of negotiating effectively than a union leader who has to rely upon demagogy and threats of strikes as a substitute for organisational efficiency.

The future growth and development of the unions in Africa depend a great deal upon an adequate flow of funds, but finance alone will not ensure stability and strength. Much the most important factor is the development of a 'cadre' of effective leaders whose principal loyalty and attachment is to the union.

In the early stages of trade-union development when the characteristic behaviour pattern is the protest demonstration, the successful union leader must possess appropriate qualities. He must be able to attract and maintain the support of the workers in the face of a hostile response from employers and governments. His initial task is to gain recognition for the union and to make it a force to be reckoned with. In the first phase of union development the requirements of leadership are primarily demagogic. Later, when an organisation has been created and a system of industrial relations established, the qualities needed are more bureaucratic. The leader must be able to administer and to negotiate as well as to inspire and stimulate.

In most African countries the first generation union leaders have also been politicians. The achievement of independence as a goal to be sought by the union has been inseparable from the winning of better wages and working conditions. The building up of a system of collective bargaining and the achievement of independence are not, however, identical processes. The importance attached to the achievement of political objectives inevitably detracted from the development of the unions as organisations and shifted attention away from their industrial functions.

Where, however, the union was established on the basis of an

32

enterprise, as was often the case in the former British territories in Africa, the emphasis placed on their industrial functions was markedly greater than where the unions were national organisations, or part of an ideologically motivated federation. In the former case, leaders were often clerical employees who had acquired the bureaucratic skills and social ambitions to found a union. They were able, over the course of time, to establish negotiating relations with the employers for whom their members worked. They could not and did not remain entirely aloof from political affiliations and activities, but their primary concern was to secure an improvement in the terms and conditions of employment of their members. Some of them were also highly concerned with their own aggrandizement and a few have made not inconsiderable financial gains from skilfully exploiting their control of union funds and their close relations with employers and governments.

Thus the type of leadership that has emerged has been related to the character and function of the trade union organisation, and the role that the unions have played in the various countries. The nature of union leadership has inevitably changed over time. With the recognition of unions, the building up of a structured system of industrial relations and the change in political context brought about by the attainment of independence, the function and pattern of leadership has altered. The change in leadership behaviour has not always been immediate or well adapted, but it has taken place in significant respects. The present generation of union leaders is compelled by contemporary circumstances to pay more attention to union administration and industrial negotiation than its predecessor. Unions are expected to support governments in power, and not to exert such pressure as to create economic and political instability. To this extent union leaders continue to have an important political role to play, but it is very different from that which they played during the period before independence was achieved.

The bargaining power of the unions is thus constrained by two factors :

(1) weakness in organisation, leadership and funds ;
(2) government policy.

In spite of these limitations, as will be seen later, they have secured many remarkably good agreements. If the unions were stronger in those sectors of employment that at present are not covered by agreements, this would broaden the protection they are able to give to workers. Improved organisation would also enable the unions to play a more effective part in ensuring that agreements and protective legislation were properly carried out and administered. At the present time many unions are highly dependent upon the goodwill of the employer, who is often anxious to help the union develop as a stable, well-led organisation, since a weak union with inefficient leadership is generally irresponsible in its behaviour. The creation of a body of capable, experienced local and national leaders is the essential requirement that has to be fulfilled before this situation can be changed. It is worth adding, however, that many unions in highly developed countries owe a great deal to the assistance of employers.

There are many different situations in the African countries and the role of the unions and the freedom that they enjoy varies considerably. There can, for example, be no question that since independence there has been, so far, much greater freedom for the unions to develop as they themselves choose in Nigeria than in Ghana or Guinea. Much discussion is going on about the exact role that the unions ought to occupy, but there is as yet no unanimity as to what this should be. In most African countries the desire is to have organisationally strong unions that are politically subordinated to the government. An important question for the future is whether it is possible to achieve both of these objectives at the same time. It might be argued that this in fact has been achieved in Ghana. It could also equally well be argued that standards of employment, every bit as good as in Ghana, have been negotiated by unions elsewhere without the benefit of the type of trade union structure or the legal intervention introduced in that country.

As industrialisation proceeds, the functional need for work-people to be represented by trade unions grows. Not only is a system of representation required in the establishment of wages and working conditions, but it is also necessary for the purpose of resolving the thousand and one complications and issues that arise out of the every-day working relationships. In the stress that has been placed upon the political role of trade unions in African countries there is a danger that the perhaps more mundane, but nevertheless vital, aspect of trade union work in the enterprise is overlooked. Here again there are considerable differences between the British and French methods of handling these functions. In the French system of industrial relations, problems arising at the place of work are commonly handled by *délégués du personnel* elected by requirement under the

# The Trade Unions

*Code du Travail* who may not be union officials or even have union membership. Thus the unions in France and in the former French territories are encouraged by the legal regulation of industrial relations to concentrate on problems external to the firm — whereas in Britain and the former British territories the opposite is the case. Thus the emphasis on the role of the union in the plant and hence the pattern of collective bargaining and the scope and content of collective agreements is different.

35

Chapter 3

# THE EMPLOYERS

THE attitude and behaviour manifested by governments and private employers towards the organisation of labour has been the same in Africa as in the industrially more advanced countries at similar stages of their economic and social development. The initial response of governments and private employers to the emergence of trade unions and collective demands for improvements in wages and working conditions was one of hostility. Governments were fearful that unions would cause disruption and give rise to acute political and economic problems ; private employers were outraged by the temerity of their employees, who had challenged their prerogative to determine the terms and conditions on which a man was to be employed. Employers believed that to accede to the demands of the unions would be tantamount to giving up their right and authority to manage ; they feared that the consequence would be economic ruin and they expected the Government to support their view.

The first stages in the development of a modern system of industrial relations in which workers were able to bring pressure to bear upon the Government and private employers through collective organisation were inevitably stormy. In this respect there has been no difference in the history of the evolution of industrial relations in Africa from that of the older and today industrially more advanced countries. There has, however, been a difference in the speed at which governments and employers in Africa have advanced from their fairly hostile response to becoming the initiators of a modern system of industrial relations. The rapidity of this transition owes a great deal to the fact that African countries were the colonial territories of advanced industrial nations. The British and French Governments, under pressure from their own well organised labour movements, applied the principles and procedures that had become established and endorsed by international opinion to their territories overseas.[1] A little later the large British and European privately owned companies began to adapt their labour policies to the changing

[1] See B. C. Roberts, *op. cit.*

political and social situation. They recognised trade unions and began to conclude collective agreements.

## GOVERNMENTS AS EMPLOYERS

Governments have exercised a dual influence on the development of collective bargaining. In the first place they have been responsible for the introduction of legislation designed to encourage the growth of trade unions and to regulate the relations between unions and employers. In the course of administering this legislation through Labour Departments, they have exercised a continuous influence on industrial relations. In the second place, as the main employers in most African countries, governments have exercised an important influence on the development of collective bargaining.

We shall not, at this stage, discuss the nature and significance of the legislation introduced by governments for the purpose of regulating industrial relations ; we shall notice, however, the role of governments as employers. In this role the behaviour of governments has not infrequently been in contradiction to their legislative action. Governments in the former British territories were quite often reluctant to recognise unions of civil servants and to grant their own employees the bargaining rights private employers were expected to accord. This reluctance to be in the vanguard, displayed by colonial governments, followed exactly the pattern of behaviour of the governments of the older industrial countries at a similar stage in the development of their systems of industrial relations.[1] The common factor which explains the attitude shown by most governments to demands that they should be prepared to recognise the right of their own employees to join unions and to have their terms of employment determined by negotiation is to be found in the dislike which governments have of being compelled to make changes by outside pressures. All governments have feared that to accept a collective bargaining procedure would be to incur the danger of strikes, which they considered to be an unconstitutional and inadmissible action on the part of government servants.

Governments have also had other reasons for not accepting collective bargaining with enthusiasm. As the major employers, any change in the level of wages and salaries would have a powerful

---

[1] See S. and B. Webb, *The History of Trade Unionism*, Longmans, London, 1920 ; B. C. Roberts, *The History of the T.U.C. 1868–1921*, Allen & Unwin, London, 1958.

impact on the economy. If too great an increase was conceded a price inflation could easily be generated ; but it was perhaps not this danger, so much as the knowledge that employers in the private sector, who would have to grant the same scale of wage increase as the Government, would exert the maximum political pressure against the Government to prevent it agreeing to pay higher wages. Professor Berg, for example, cites the case of the Federation of French West Africa, which employed some 30 per cent of the labour force and also fixed the minimum wage for unskilled labour, thus indirectly fixing the wage rates of most wage earners in the country.[1] 'If, for example,' writes Berg, 'the Governor of Senegal raises the minimum wage rate by 10 per cent, the unions (or management) will insist on the same increase for graded labour in the negotiations in the Joint Councils.' Similar examples could be cited from most other territories in all parts of Africa.

Furthermore, any increase in the pay of government employees might give rise to considerable financial problems for the government. Unless revenue was rising fast from a rapid rate of economic growth, taxes would have to be raised to cover the increase in costs or a deficit would be incurred. Such a course would almost certainly involve the Government in unpopularity and might have an adverse effect upon economic development.

The problem of fixing the appropriate levels of pay for government employees under all circumstances is difficult,[2] but it is especially difficult when the consequences of a decision are as far reaching as they have been in most African territories.

In most of the former British territories, following the end of the Second World War, governments agreed under pressure from London to the establishment of joint (Whitley) councils for the purpose of discussing all questions concerned with conditions of employment.[3] There were, however, many complaints from the unions of civil servants that governments were not especially good employers and that they did not make adequate efforts to ensure that the Whitley Councils worked successfully. Nevertheless, there was

[1] Elliot Berg, 'French West Africa' in W. Galenson (ed.), *Labour and Economic Development*, John Wiley, New York, 1959.
[2] The problem in Britain and France during the post-war period bears eloquent testimony to this fact. See H. M. Douty, 'Salary Determination for White-Collar Civil Servants in Great Britain', *Monthly Labour Review*, November 1960.
[3] See *Report on Methods of Negotiation between the Government and Government Employees on Questions affecting Conditions of Service in Industrial Departments* (Lagos, 1948).

a continuing dialogue between the governments and the representatives of their employees.

Although wages were the most important issue discussed, it could hardly be claimed that negotiations on claims by the governments' employees were outstandingly successful. In most cases, owing to the difficulty of financing an increase in costs and the possible effect on the levels of wages in the private sector, governments refused to concede the claims pursued through the Whitley Councils, until the pressure mounted to the point where it was necessary to establish a special Commission of Inquiry. This was often conducted by a distinguished person from the United Kingdom. In the end an increase in pay would be recommended and the government concerned would agree to make some improvement.

In the French-speaking countries civil servants were members of trade unions and there was consultation with the governments. As in the British territories there was a reluctance to raise pay until a point had been reached where the pressures were no longer containable. There were no collective agreements covering civil servants, and the procedures laid down in the *Code du Travail* of 1952 did not apply to the governments' own employees. However, they did apply to employees of public utilities such as electricity supply, water supply, railways and docks.

Since independence, the role of Government as an employer has become more important in both English- and French-speaking countries. In general, however, the change from colonial status has made relatively little difference. Governments are still extremely concerned about the impact of wage increases on the general level of costs and are no more ready to give way to the claims of their employees than they were hitherto.

In Ghana, since the passing of the Industrial Relations Act in 1958, civil servants, local government employees and teachers have not been eligible for a bargaining certificate and therefore they have no right to insist that the Government should negotiate, nor have they any right to strike. However, the junior grades of civil servants are permitted to have representatives on Joint Advisory Committees which may discuss conditions of service. There is also a good deal of informal consultation with the unions which cover employees of the Government, but it is doubtful if these organisations are in a position to exercise strong pressure.

39

## THE PRIVATE EMPLOYER

The rise of trade unions and the pressure for increased wages and better working conditions inevitably compelled employers to revise their labour policies. They naturally responded in different ways according to their situation. After they had passed the stage where it was no longer possible to refuse to bargain with unions, the major employers in the former British territories began to adjust in two ways. They developed much more sophisticated policies of labour management and they joined together in associations to present a common front to the unions and to bring pressure to bear upon the governments.

The labour policies of the large international companies have today fully accepted that they cannot settle the conditions of employment of their workers unilaterally. They have entered into union recognition agreements ; allowed union representatives access to their employees ; agreed to check-off union contributions ; and are prepared to negotiate on as wide a range of issues as any company in Europe or the U.S.A.

Some companies are highly paternalistic as are some companies in the older industrial countries. In many cases they show considerable good will towards the unions, partly because they do not wish to be labelled as anti-union, but also because they genuinely believe that if they pursue fair and conciliatory policies they will induce a positive response from the unions. They much prefer to have stable industrial relations and a co-operative labour force, than to save a penny at the cost of strikes and industrial unrest. In many cases when important negotiations are to take place, advice will be tendered from the company's headquarters and it is not uncommon for a senior official to be sent out to Africa to take charge of the actual negotiations. As a result of these developments the standard of collective bargaining has been raised to a level far above the crude battle that used to take place twenty years ago when unions and employers first faced each other to settle a demand for higher pay and better working conditions.

The number of enterprises which can be said to have reached this standard are, of course, relatively few, but they include the largest and from the economic point of view the most important employers in the English-speaking countries. Many of the smaller and indigenous employers display a less sympathetic attitude to unions and such bargaining as takes place follows a more difficult path.

## EMPLOYERS' ASSOCIATIONS

Employers' associations have become increasingly important in the former British territories, in spite of the fact that collective agreements are mainly negotiated upon an enterprise basis. This development has much in common with the development of employers' associations that took place in Britain towards the end of the 19th century. Employers were then persuaded to join together in order to bring their influence more effectively to bear upon the Government and to counter the growing demands of the unions for industry-wide agreements. In the African as well as in all the other former British territories overseas, employers have seen an advantage in having an association that could voice their interests and present a common front to the unions.

These associations have been of two types. One kind has been the association of employers in a particular field of economic activity, for example associations of coffee, tea and sisal producers in East Africa, or of mining companies in West Africa, Zambia and Rhodesia. In addition to these industry associations there is in each territory an association representing all employers.

Where an industry association of employers exists there has generally been a trend towards industry-wide agreements. For example, the Kenya Coffee Growers' Association has negotiated an agreement with the Kenya Coffee Plantation Workers' Union; in Tanzania the Sisal Growers' Association has agreements with the Plantation Workers' Union.

In some cases, for example, in the Zambia copper-mining industry, the employers present a common front to the unions, but the agreements are signed separately by each of the companies. Though there is no single industry-wide agreement the net effect of the employers' joint policy is the same. When disputes have occurred they have sometimes been arbitrated or inquired into on the basis of the entire copper-mining industry.[1]

The function of the central Employers' Federation in each country is not to negotiate agreements, though they may well assist member firms or associations in this activity, but to act as a centre of information and for the co-ordination of policy so far as this is possible.

[1] See, for example, *The Report and Award of the Arbitrator C. W. Guillebaud Esq., C.B.E., nominated under the Industrial Conciliation Ordinance to arbitrate in a dispute between the Northern Rhodesia African Mineworkers' Trade Union and the Copper Mining Companies, January, 1953*, Department of Labour, Lusaka. Also, *Report of the Commission Appointed to Inquire into the Mining Industry in Northern Rhodesia*, Lusaka, 1962.

Much of their work is concerned with the representation of the employers' views to the Government on matters of common interest. In this respect they act as the counterpart of the central trade union bodies; thus assisting in the development of a consultative and pressure group system of industrial democracy.

Many of the associations publish regular news letters for the purpose of keeping their members informed on current trends and developments. Most of them are affiliated to the Organisation of Employers' Federations and Employers in Developing Countries, which has its headquarters in London. Through this affiliation they are kept in touch with developments in other countries, including both those in the early stages of economic development and those who have reached advanced levels of industrial development. The Organisation of Employers' Federations, formerly called the Overseas Employers' Federation, was of great importance before the African countries became independent, since it was in a position to consult with the British Government on matters that affected the interests of employers in the colonial territories.[1] The Overseas Employers' Federation was also in close contact with the British Trades' Union Congress and with the various international agencies including the ILO.

The influence of the OEF on the evolution of employment policies in the member firms of affiliated associations was considerable. However, unlike the situation in France, the OEF was never able to dictate the policy of either the industry or national associations. Through its publications, meetings and conferences, and the visits of its staff, it was able to bring an informed and enlightened influence to bear. For example, the Federation's careful analysis of the advantages and disadvantages of the 'check-off' system did a good deal to show employers that stable trade unionism was to their benefit as well as to the benefit of their employees.[2]

The weakness in the present pattern of employers' organisations is that they are mainly confined to the British and other overseas firms that are established in English-speaking countries. There are signs, however, that indigenous local employers are coming to realise the advantage of belonging to an association. Many of the small employers are reluctant to belong, because they do not see their interests as identical with those of the larger firms. Moreover, since

[1] For a discussion of the history and development of the role of the Overseas Employers' Federation, see B. C. Roberts, *op. cit.*

[2] See *Deduction of Union Dues by the Employer* (*Check-off*), Overseas Employers Federation Occasional Paper 1961.

many of them do not negotiate with trade unions, they see no value in belonging to an employers' association. In this respect they behave no differently from countless small employers in the more advanced industrial countries, who also are able to avoid bargaining with unions and who see no identity of interest with the large companies and therefore no advantage in belonging to an employers' association.

Employers' associations in the English-speaking African countries are entirely voluntary bodies. They cannot compel a member firm to carry out their policy or recommendations. It could be argued that this limited authority wielded by the employers' association executive is also a source of weakness when the general trend is towards more centralisation in political and economic decision-making. Such a conclusion could be subject to the criticism that a concentration of power in the hands of a small number of employers' leaders might bring greater uniformity at the expense of stifling the new developments and flexible adjustments that a rapidly developing economy ought to be making.

In the former Federation of French West Africa most trading and commercial enterprises were members of the Syndicat des Commerçants, Importateurs - Exportateurs (SCIMPEX); while industrial and construction firms belonged to the Union Intersyndicale d'Entreprises et d'Industrie de l'A.O.F. (UNISYNDI). Both of these organisations, as in the case of their counterparts the trade unions, were off-shoots of parent organisations in France and their activities were closely supervised by the Centre National du Patronat Français (CNPF). The control exercised over the policy and actions of SCIMPEX from France was quite rigorous. Any agreement that it might propose to make on wages or on any other matter was subject to approval from Paris or Marseilles. It was, in fact, impossible for even a detail to be modified without the securing of telegraphic authorisation from France. UNISYNDI enjoyed a somewhat greater degree of freedom of action from metropolitan control. Attempts were made to bring about a merger of the two organisations, but these came to naught. However, in spite of this failure to bring about a unification, the two organisations worked closely together.

After independence was granted and the Federations broke up, the employers' organisations were regrouped in each country. Today, the separation between SCIMPEX and UNISYNDI exists only in Senegal, where, however, the two bodies have developed a very close relationship. A major change has been the severing of all organic ties with the employers' organisations in France. The

43

changed situation is reflected in the organisational structure which has been developed since independence. The unified employers' association in each country is now a body that represents African firms, even though these might be owned by parent companies domiciled in Europe or elsewhere overseas. The officers of the employers' associations in each country are no longer appointed and paid by the parent organisations in France as used to be the case. Nor does the CNPF exercise any control over these national organisations as it did in the days before independence. There is in existence a body which is called the Association Interprofessionnelle de l'Afrique tropicale (AIAT) which is located in Paris and acts as an information and advising centre for the national employers' associations. This body takes great care not to give the impression that it is in any way attempting to dictate the policy of the national bodies it represents. Instead, it seeks to encourage all member firms and the national associations to which they belong, to adapt themselves to the local situation which prevails. The work of the AIAT is more important in the economic field than in the field of industrial relations. It is mostly by means of consultation with governments that employers make their influence felt. Since each association represents all the employers in the country, the governments consult them willingly on such issues as raising the national minimum wage (SMIG) or making a change in labour codes. At times the AIAT is itself asked to give an opinion to a government concerned with an important policy change.

The determination of both parties to prevent wage increases from undermining economic stability by restrictive measures has been a factor contributing to the establishment of smooth relations between employers' associations and governments, even in those countries most emphatically seeking to become socialist states. However, the opposition to excessive wage increases pursued by the employers' associations does not seem to prevent an individual member from taking, on his own initiative and often with semi-official support, steps to increase pay made necessary by rises in the cost of living. Thus, while employers have taken care to co-operate with governments they have not given up all freedom of action and it is quite clear that this situation meets with the approval of most governments. On the other hand, the limitations imposed by certain governments, such as that of Mali, on the right of an employer to dismiss a worker is a more onerous restriction and gives rise to private complaint. Thus, by and large, employers and their associations have accepted the new regimes and changes in policy which they have introduced and in so doing have helped to maintain the considerable element of continuity in the broad pattern of industrial relations.

Employers in both English- and French-speaking countries of Africa, after an initial period of hostility to the development of trade unions, have played a positive role in the evolution of the systems of industrial relations which have emerged. They have come to accept that wages and other conditions of employment are most effectively settled by a process of discussion between responsible representatives. Employers in the former British territories, whilst showing a preference for autonomous collective bargaining, have also accepted the fact that under the economic and social conditions prevailing in most African countries, the State has a much larger role to play than in the traditional British system of industrial relations. French employers, who have been used to determining the terms and conditions of employment of their workers in the context of a far greater degree of State regulation, have found no difficulty in accepting the extension of the pattern established in their country of origin to the French-speaking countries of Africa.

Chapter 4

# COLLECTIVE BARGAINING

A COLLECTIVE agreement regulating the terms and conditions of employment may be adopted in a number of different ways. At one end of the scale it may be reached at the end of negotiations between a trade union and an employers' association within a legal framework which gives to both parties the maximum degree of freedom to settle their differences on mutually acceptable terms. At the other end of the scale collective agreements may be drafted by a Department of Government, as part of the process of the administration of economic and social policy ; the agreements are legally binding upon unions and employers who are obliged to carry out their terms.

The extreme cases are easily recognised, but the difficult question to decide is exactly at what point collective bargaining ceases to exist and is superseded by the process of administration.

In principle, the right of employers and unions to bargain collectively over the terms and conditions of employment is not contested in any of the countries under survey. The advantages of a method of determining the terms and conditions of employment which is based upon the consent of the interested parties and which takes account of the factors that are peculiar to each branch of production and unit of employment are widely recognised. But the acceptance of collective bargaining as a matter of principle, as the acceptance of the principle of freedom of association, leaves considerable latitude for interpretation.

As noted earlier, certain conditions must be fulfilled before collective bargaining can take place. There must be representative organisations of employees, which must be independent of the employer with whom they are negotiating on behalf of their members. If the union is totally dependent upon the employer as in the case of the 'company unions' which existed at various stages in the development of the older industrialised countries, there cannot be genuine collective bargaining. The relationship in such circumstances is not one of equals, but of subordinate to superior.

In the African countries examined in this survey, the unions are free from total economic dependence upon employers, but they are often in a position where the goodwill and even assistance of the employer is not an unimportant factor. It is difficult to evaluate the extent to which this goodwill influences the outcome of collective bargaining in African countries. All that can be said is that there is not much reason to believe that this factor is always of greater significance than it is in the more advanced industrial countries.

The organisation of independent trade unions is only the first step in the development of a collective bargaining system. Before bargaining can take place a union must be recognised by an employer as a legitimate bargaining agent. The achievement of recognition has been a matter of demonstrating the strength of the union's claim to represent the employees concerned. In the early days of union activity this was generally won after a bitter struggle, often involving strikes and not infrequently violence. The difficulty of building union strength to the level where it could effectively persuade employers to grant recognition voluntarily was recognised in the public policy of the British and French Governments during the colonial period. Systems of State intervention ranging from the exercise of persuasive pressure by Departments of Labour to the making of union recognition compulsory have been used as a substitute for union strength.

In general it has been in the English-speaking countries that voluntary persuasion has been relied upon as the most effective method of establishing a viable collective bargaining system. In most of these countries voluntary recognition and the willingness to bargain has been consolidated by collective agreements establishing the rights of the parties concerned. In some countries the voluntary approach has given way, since they achieved independence, to a legal obligation on employers to recognise unions and to bargain with them in good faith. In certain instances this legal establishment of bargaining rights has been supplemented by the introduction of a system of compulsory arbitration, thus limiting their exercise to a pattern approved by Government policy.

In French-speaking countries, the free bargaining system, if not unknown, plays but a small role. The procedure for the achievement of collective agreements is in fact close to an administrative process. It confers on the public authorities a decisive role in the conduct of negotiations. Unions and employers have their part to play, but the outcome of what is in practice compulsory negotiation is to a great extent the product of a system in which the State is the dominant partner.

Before examining in greater detail the principal systems involved, it should be pointed out that the differences between them are the result of differences not only in the philosophy of industrial relations, but also in the techniques employed. In Africa these are not the products of indigenous invention, but have been imported in the main from Britain and France and to a lesser degree from the U.S.A., Germany and elsewhere. These techniques, from the moment they are introduced, undergo more or less important modifications as they are fitted into local context. Eventually they become solidly welded into the juridical and institutional fabric of the countries concerned. None the less, the systems of industrial relations in force in all the African countries are strongly branded by the traditions from which they spring. The influence in particular of Anglo-Saxon and French patterns of thought and institutional developments has been most marked, and in what follows we shall be mainly concerned with the evolution of collective bargaining in the former British and French African countries.

## I. COLLECTIVE BARGAINING IN ENGLISH-SPEAKING COUNTRIES

In the English-speaking countries collective bargaining has been developed as the central feature of their systems of industrial relations. This was the object of British policy in the field of industrial relations from the earliest days of its formulation more than thirty years ago. Even before local legislation had been introduced, employers were encouraged to follow paths already well trod in Britain. As laws to regulate the development of trade unions and their relations with employers were adopted, they were based upon British Acts of Parliament.

There were inevitably some changes. These changes were designed to regulate the activities of newly born unions more closely than was the case in the United Kingdom until such time as they had learned to operate effectively and responsibly on a voluntary basis. Since independence, there have been departures from this concept of transitional regulation and new and more restrictive laws match a new conception of the role of the public authorities. In these cases there has been an important shift in objective. Doubt has been cast upon the basic assumption made by the British authorities that in the final analysis a voluntary system of collective bargaining would produce the most satisfactory results from the point of view of the interests of individual workers, employers and the State. None the less, in most of these territories and countries the original foundations remain largely intact, in so far as they affect bargaining procedure and the settlement of disputes. This means that by and large the State has not taken over the function of determining the pattern of bargaining when the parties have proved capable of establishing their own procedures ; and that when disputes occur it offers its good offices and only in the last resort prevents them from producing their extreme consequences. In some cases there is un-doubtedly a disposition to go further and to establish fully fledged systems of socialist planning based upon the complete public owner-ship of the entire means of production and distribution. However, no former British territory has reached anywhere near such a point of development and in the political, social and economic circum-stances which at present prevail it is unlikely that an all-embracing State-regulated system of industrial relations could be effectively established even if it were thought desirable. Thus even in the countries that have moved farthest away from the British pattern there is still much of it discernible.

## The Recognition of Trade Unions

Collective bargaining brings up at the outset a problem in labour-management relations that is unknown in the French-speaking countries, namely, the *recognition* of the trade union as an institution qualified to represent its members. This problem, which has arisen in all the English-speaking countries, though not always to the same degree, stems from the basic British attitude to the fundamental rights of workers and employers and the associations to which they belong.

In Britain, union recognition has always been a voluntary matter. Employers have been legally free to recognise or not to recognise a union for bargaining purposes ; they are also free to make union membership a condition of employment or to refuse to employ any person who belongs to a union. The objective that the legislature and the courts have sought to attain in British law has been the removal of legal obstacles to organisation and bargaining. The principle of negative protection, as a means of giving positive support to the development of trade unions and collective bargaining, was extended to all the colonial territories while they were under British rule.

Whereas employers in the French-speaking territories are prevented by law from refusing to negotiate with an organisation that the Government considers as representative of a given group of employees, in most English-speaking countries there is nothing to oblige them to treat a trade union as a valid partner, even if it is duly registered. The problem of recognition, therefore, becomes one of union strength together with the willingness of employers to enter into a bargaining relationship.

In all the English-speaking countries, most employers have come to accept that there are more advantages than drawbacks in recognising unions and bargaining with them. However, in many of the countries there are employers who still refuse to recognise the existence of a union and will not enter into bargaining with one. Whilst this is the case it can be said that this situation is usually to be found where the employer is a small local enterprise and the union concerned is weak and unstable. A paternalistic treatment of the staff is commonly the substitute for union recognition.

In the English-speaking countries it is common for employers to enter into a recognition agreement with a union. The nature of such agreements will be discussed later (Chapter 5), but it is necessary to say here that this agreement is designed to establish the fact that the union is truly representative of a majority of employees. A recognition agreement gives the union the status of a bargaining agent that may be obtained under different circumstances in other countries by a legal procedure. Where there is a multiplicity of trade unions the problem of recognition is complicated and some method of promoting a stable relationship is required; a recognition agreement serves this purpose.

Recognition does not necessarily imply that effective collective bargaining will take place. There are examples to be found where even unquestionably representative unions have entered into recognition agreements but have failed, through lack of resources and weak leadership or employer resistance, to negotiate further agreements covering wages and working conditions. In some of these cases employers are following a pattern of wages determined, in effect, elsewhere and the union is merely acting as an agent for the settlement of grievances.

A radical remedy for these difficulties has been provided by legislation in some of the English-speaking countries who have thus departed from the British tradition of voluntaryism. Ghana, borrowing in part from United States law, introduced in the Industrial Relations Act of 1958 the principle that any trade union accepted by the TUC as representing the interests of a given category of wage earners may be granted a certificate to bargain by the Minister of Labour, who may further approve the establishment of appropriate bargaining machinery. A union in possession of a bargaining certificate may compel an employer to commence negotiations by serving a notice upon him to this effect. Refusal to comply entails penal sanctions. Such compulsion has hardly ever been formally applied, since permanent bargaining machinery was set up. Employers in Ghana no longer refuse on principle to consider the claims of their employees, but unions are not allowed to strike to enforce a decision that is favourable to themselves without going through a restraining procedure. A deadlock in negotiation must be reported to the Department of Labour for conciliation and if this fails it may be sent ultimately to arbitration.

In Sudan an Act of 1960 on labour disputes lays down that the parties to a dispute over employment conditions must negotiate. If there is no properly constituted trade union, two-thirds of the workers may submit a request for an amicable settlement to the Commissioner for Labour. This possibility prevents an employer from ignoring the demands of his staff disqualifying their representatives as acceptable negotiators. Ethiopia has started to follow a similar path by a decree issued in 1962, under which 'each party engaged in collective bargaining shall be required to recognise all the other parties thereto and to negotiate with them in good faith'. Tanzania has also decided to break with the British tradition and has placed its industrial relations system on a new legal basis.

The other English-speaking countries have so far refrained from changing their law so as to provide a legal solution to the problem of union recognition and collective bargaining. The development of employers' associations has been a favourable factor in bringing about the general recognition of trade unions. Since these associations have come into existence as a response to the growth of trade unions, they have a common interest in the development of collective bargaining arrangements. Although their function is to represent the interests of the employers in negotiations, they have sought to put their relations with the unions on a firmly established procedural basis. A good example of this type of development is to be found in

51

the Industrial Relations Charter agreed to by the Government of Kenya, the Federation of Kenya Employers and the Kenya Federation of Labour in October 1962.[1]

The fact that there is no law compelling an employer to recognise a union and to bargain in good faith does not mean that the public authorities exercise no influence. From the 1920s it was the policy of the British Government to encourage union development and to persuade employers to accept collective bargaining as the best way of determining wages and conditions of employment. Departments of Labour have continuously pressed employers to follow this policy. In some countries the Government has sought to make the problem of union recognition less difficult by using the procedure of compulsory registration to check the rise of rival organisations, by making it difficult for new unions to gain registration where the workers in a plant or sector of industry were already adequately represented. The decision of the Registrar was usually open to appeal to a court of justice. Nevertheless this limitation on the right to organise has given rise to problems of conformity with the International Labour Code.[2]

There can be little doubt that where unions are reasonably strong they generally have little problem of recognition in most of the English-speaking countries at the present time. There are, however, many small-scale employers who are able to avoid bargaining with unions and they will be able to continue to do so until union organisations are very much stronger and more effectively organised. For this reason it is likely that unions in those countries which have not changed their laws to provide for compulsory recognition and the right to bargain will tend to press for this development. There seems to be little doubt after a few years' experience, in spite of reservations in other respects, that this change in the law in Ghana did substantially strengthen the position of the unions and improve industrial relations by putting to an end disputes over recognition. However, it must be added that a change of this kind will not of itself ensure that there is effective union bargaining. In this respect there has been much controversy in the United States.[3] The extent to which

[1] See Appendix I.
[2] In 1962 Sierra Leone, following observations by the ILO Committee of Experts on the application of Conventions and Recommendations amended its Trade Unions Act so as to remove the provision empowering the Registrar to refuse the registration of a new trade union if there was already an existing union catering for a similar group of workers. Report III, Part IV, ILO, 1964, p. 132.
[3] Philip Ross, *The Government as a Source of Union Power*, Brown University Press, 1965.

positive protection does make for stronger unions and successful collective bargaining depends upon so many other factors that it is impossible to give a completely categorical answer to those who doubt the wisdom of this type of legal support.

## The Level of Negotiations

In the English-speaking countries legislatures have, as a rule, limited the use of their powers to defining how the government might intervene if the parties concerned were unable to reach agreement. In other words the laws in force in most of these countries provide hardly more than the outlines of a procedure for settling labour disputes. Only rarely are precise rules for the normal course of negotiations stipulated. The result in the English-speaking countries is a great diversity as regards both the way in which negotiations are carried on and the level at which they are undertaken. The difference is great, where the French-speaking countries are concerned, as each has adopted a similar code of law setting up a rigid machinery for the negotiation of collective agreements.

The logical outcome of a system in which collective agreements owe something to the part played by the authorities in drafting them, have some of the force of law and are, so to say, an extension of it, is centralised bargaining. Hence in the French-speaking countries there is a high degree of uniformity in the structure and pattern of collective bargaining. Conversely, when there is no such principle of uniformity and administrative influence at work and the basic concept of negotiation is to fix acceptable conditions of employment to the parties concerned in the light of a given situation, the normal bargaining unit will be empirically determined. And this is what we find in the majority of English-speaking countries.

The pattern of trade-union organisation has tended to favour the emergence of a variety of bargaining units. In many cases union organisation has been based upon the enterprise and this naturally has set the limit of the agreement. In those cases where the enterprise has been large or its activities spread over a number of plants, there may well have been a multiplicity of unions involved, each preferring to negotiate its own agreement. However, in certain sectors of employment, such as Government departments, docks, railways and even mines, there have been in existence from a comparatively early period industry-wide unions which have negotiated industry-wide agreements.

In certain instances industry-wide agreements have been promoted by the establishment, as in Sierra Leone, of wages boards. Though it would be going too far to assert that industry-wide bargaining has become the dominant form in the English-speaking countries of Africa, there has been something of a trend in this direction. The consolidation of unions and employers' organisations has tended to encourage the placing of negotiations in a broader framework than that of the plant or even the enterprise. In this respect there have been interesting developments in East Africa. Each of the four major branches of agriculture in Kenya is covered by a single agreement, which since 1963 it has been the task of the United Agricultural Workers' Union to renew. The same is true of the extensive sugar-cane plantations of Uganda. Tanzania too, even before the trade union reform of 1964, offered an example of centralised bargaining in the agricultural sector. In the public services which are of common interest to these three countries and are managed by a Federal body, working conditions are the subject of regular bargaining at the level of the Federation.

Although the trade-union structure has been thoroughly rationalised in Ghana, bargaining takes place on the enterprise as well as on an industry- or service-wide basis. Unions may be negotiating for a common group of employees with a number of employers and the same type of multi-employer bargaining is to be found in the copper-mining industry of Zambia. In the latter case, each of the unions concerned is bargaining for the classes of workers it represents with nine companies as if they were a single employer, yet each agreement, though identical in content, is legally distinct. In other cases, although the agreements take the shape of plant or enterprise agreements, the actual situation is closer to that of an industry-wide agreement since the situation is one in which a single firm occupies a dominating position. Nigeria, where bargaining is predominantly of the enterprise pattern, offers more than one example of this type of situation.

The development of industry-wide agreements in the English-speaking countries has followed a similar path to that which occurred in Britain as unions and employers extended the scope and scale of their organisation. The pattern is, however, likely to remain mixed, since the economic and structural factors differ considerably from industry to industry.[1] Centralised bargaining may in fact have

[1] This situation can be observed, for instance in Kenya, where in the insurance field 17 companies operating under very diverse conditions were governed in 1963 by different agreements, whereas in the case of the banks a unified procedure had been achieved.

serious disadvantages, since, when it is necessary to satisfy the needs of enterprises of widely varying financial standing, discussion becomes laborious and prolonged and sometimes no agreement at all is possible.[1] In many cases, however, these problems may be only temporary, for they are frequently linked with circumstances that are passing, especially when differences in policy have arisen from whether the staff of a firm was African or not.[2] Moreover, some of the difficulties will be mitigated if negotiations undertaken at the level of industry are restricted to problems of general interest, leaving those of local interest to be solved by complementary agreements negotiated by management and trade unions in the undertaking or plants concerned. Several agreements already concluded at the level of the industry stipulate a procedure for the joint settlement at the local level of a number of questions requiring detailed consideration, such as productivity bonuses, working hours and holidays, safety measures and disciplinary issues. In a number of countries this approach has led to the drafting of general agreements for industries as a whole which, like those in the French-speaking countries, broadly determine the major conditions of employment, while wages and certain other elements continue to be the object of local agreements negotiated at the level of the branch of industry or the enterprise.

The trend towards centralised bargaining will almost certainly be accentuated with the industrial and economic development of the countries under survey. But the most important influence will probably be that of Government policy. The trend towards industry-wide agreements was most obviously accelerated in Britain during the First World War when the Government was concerned to impose a general economic policy on industry. Since Government planning and the application of over-all economic and social policies are likely to become a more significant feature of developing countries in the future, bargaining procedures will inevitably be moulded to match this development.

## The Bargaining Machinery

The structure of collective bargaining in the English-speaking countries of Africa is widely varied. It has been shaped by the belief that while an orderly procedure is important, uniformity is less

---

[1] An example of such difficulties could be observed in the case of the food-processing industries in Kenya.

[2] Differences of this kind seem to have been one of the factors preventing the conclusion of a single agreement covering all Nairobi insurance companies.

important than mutual understanding and accommodation. Following British practice, unions and employees have established by voluntary agreement joint negotiating committees or joint industrial councils in many industries and undertakings. In addition to this formal procedural framework, many supplementary arrangements have been devised to provide for a discussion of matters at issue between employers and workers. These may involve highly formal procedures or no more than an undertaking by management, after informal discussions, to concede a claim made on an *ad hoc* basis. Improvements in conditions of employment induced by union pressure might simply be recorded in a letter from management to inform the union of its decision, and subsequently the new conditions might be embodied in a staff handbook side by side with other regulations that were never negotiated.[1] Where joint consultative committees exist there may be a substantial element of bargaining between management and the representatives of the workers under the guise of a mutual exchange of views. Sometimes there may be a long-drawn-out process of negotiation going through a well recognised procedure and ending in a carefully drawn up agreement accepted by both parties.

The establishment of Wages Boards and Wages Councils by law in the English-speaking territories was the only exception to the principle of industrial self-regulation, which left the form the negotiations procedures should take entirely to the parties, until the Ghana Industrial Relations Act of 1958. Under the Wages Boards Ordinance of Sierra Leone, for example, the Governor in Council, if satisfied that the conditions of employment or other circumstances of any groups of workers were such as to render expedient the establishment of a Wages Board, was empowered to set one up. However, before so doing the Governor was obliged to give notice of his intention and to give consideration to any objection that might be lodged in writing within a period of forty days. If in the opinion of the Governor the objections were such as to make it inadvisable to proceed with the proposal he must make this fact known by an official notice. Similar provisions are still in force in a number of countries. Thus, although the establishment of a Wages Board is an administrative act, it is only done in consultation with the parties concerned and

---

[1] Thus the salaries and other working conditions of the technical and administrative staffs of the Zambian mines are not fixed by a collective agreement in the strict sense of the term, but by a sort of regulation, each of whose points is under constant review by management under pressure from the unions and changes in the labour market.

would not be imposed against their joint opposition.

Wages Boards have been likened to a crutch to collective bargaining, rather than a substitute for it. It was certainly the intention of the labour advisors to the Colonial Governments that they should only be established in the absence of effective voluntary machinery and that in their functioning they would be a preparation for an eventual transformation to a Joint Industrial Council. Hence Wages Boards are composed of representatives of trade unions and employers from the area or the industry covered, with the addition of a small number of public members, one of whom is nominated Chairman and another Deputy Chairman by the Governor. A Wages Board has the power to fix the minimum rate of wages, hours of work, overtime rates and holidays with pay, for all or any group of workers within the jurisdiction of the Board. The normal procedure of a Wages Board is to meet when required to consider a proposal from either the employers or union representatives. The usual case will be a claim for an improvement in wages or other conditions of employment made by the union concerned. The role of the independent members is essentially to help the two sides find a basis for an agreement which can be supported by a majority of the Board. Since in the last resort this can be achieved by the independent members voting with one side or the other, they can influence each side to make concessions as otherwise they might find themselves outvoted. Thus, it is argued, Wages Boards provide a good training in the art of necessary compromise which is an essential feature of the collective bargaining process. In this concept of bargaining the independent members are acting as conciliators, but they may in the last resort in effect have to act as arbitrators by choosing to side with either the employers or the unions, in order to reach a decision. Once a majority decision has been reached, it is conveyed to the Minister of Labour, who may, if he feels that the decision is not well founded, ask the Board to reconsider. If after they have done this and they have come to the same conclusion as before, the Minister would normally confirm the decision which then becomes legally binding upon all the employers covered, who may be compelled to pay any arrears and fines if they fail to observe the terms of the Wages Board's award. Thus, whilst it may be said that a Wages Board introduces an important element of administrative wage determination, its design also gives it a close affinity to the collective bargaining process. The actual way in which a Wages Board works depends on the desires and the will of all concerned ; it can be pulled in one direction or the other according to the wishes of its constituent elements. It is even more so in the case of Wages Councils, whose functions and powers are generally limited to a particular trade or occupation, and whose structure emphasises the part to be played by persons directly concerned with the said trade or occupation.

Other types of formal negotiating committee such as Joint Industrial Councils exist in most countries, but these are on a purely voluntary basis. The membership of these bodies, the frequency of their meetings, and the rules governing their activity are laid down in procedure agreements or in mutually accepted bye-laws drafted jointly by the organisations concerned. The size of these committees and councils varies considerably, but they are usually composed of equal numbers from each side. When required, the official representatives may be supplemented in an advisory capacity by specialists on the problems on the agenda. On the trade-union side, seats may have to be reserved for various organisations if, as sometimes happens, political or religious differences or the geographical dispersion of plants concerned prove an obstacle to homogeneous representation. Large undertakings usually appoint as their spokesmen their personnel managers or executives whose departments cover the questions under discussion. When necessary they will also take into account the need to ensure that the various plants of an enterprise or the various enterprises in the industry concerned are adequately represented. In the case of the large international oil, mining and manufacturing companies, it is not unusual for a specialist from head office to be flown out to head the negotiating team, or to act as its adviser, when important negotiations are held.

Meetings may be held at specified intervals — for instance every three months — or they may be convened at the initiative of the parties as and when desired. A widespread custom is for the chair to be occupied alternately by a member of each group, but it is sometimes allotted by common consent to the personnel manager. Rules on voting, when laid down in the rules of procedure, can vary a good deal. When a negotiating committee fails to reach a decision, the deadlock may be resolved by reference to further bodies before the parties are free to strike or lockout. One interesting method where minor questions are concerned is to refer the outstanding issue to a select committee for the special purpose of finding an acceptable solution ; this sometimes proves to be an effective way of overcoming a stubborn difficulty that threatens to prevent a broader agreement from being reached.

This principle of industrial self-regulation, which leaves the form the negotiation procedures shall take entirely to the parties — in Ghana its application is restricted by the Act of 1958 which lays down that the appointment of negotiating committees and their rules must obtain the Minister's approval — pinpoints a very important difference between these bodies and the joint commissions which exist in the French-speaking countries of western and central Africa, which like the Wages Boards or Councils in the English-speaking countries are prescribed by order of the administrative authority. Another difference from the situation in the French-speaking countries is that the power of the Department of Labour to intervene in negotiations is exercised differently. The presence of an official from the Department must be in accord with the wishes of both parties, and his role is normally discreet. He may act merely as an observer, a secretary or as an objective expert, but never as an assertive authority overriding the wishes of the parties. It has happened, of course, that while maintaining his semi-official character, he has exerted so great an influence on the course of negotiations as to warrant his being considered as a sort of informal arbitrator, even though not invited specifically to fulfil this function. As a rule, however, the Department of Labour official is careful to avoid any action justifying an allegation that the freedom of the parties has been jeopardised by pressure or directives from Government quarters. This seems to be still largely true even in countries that have established a strict control over trade-union organisations and authoritarian methods of settling disputes.[1]

Hypothetically, therefore, the course of the discussions reflects first and foremost the relative strength of the forces on each side. Needless to say, in this respect conditions vary widely from country to country and from industry to industry, from enterprise to enterprise. Some trade-union organisations, those in the Zambian copper mines for instance, have attained an authority and a bargaining power, that place them on an equal footing with the employers.

---

[1] There are various indications that in Ghana the conditions and methods of collective bargaining have not undergone the radical transformation that might have been expected after the 1958 reform. Trade-union integration is more a reality at the national level of each of the recognised organisations and at the level of the Trades Union Congress than it is at the local level ; the local leaders of the unions act more or less as do their counterparts in the countries that have maintained more liberal methods.

Sudan's experience is too limited and that of Tanzania too recent to permit the drawing of clear conclusions in this field, though mention must be made of the provisions of the Tanzanian Act of 1964 which stipulates that the trade unions must negotiate wage agreements in keeping with the national wages policy.

But there are still many cases where the unions are poorly organised and where the workers' representatives lack the ability to match the employers in negotiating skill. In these circumstances, bargaining is often little more than a statement of grievances, presented with more vehemence than method, which does little to shake the position of the other party. The problem is by no means entirely on the side of the unions. Many small and medium-sized employers fear the strength of the unions and the power of local leaders to inflame opinion and create unrest among their employees. They sometimes reflect their fear by taking up intransigent positions ; others display a contempt which is provocative. The representatives of the large companies often find themselves in the dilemma of not being sure whether the Government policy they are urged to bear in mind is really to the good of their companies. There is thus in the bargaining tactics in most of the countries the reflection of a good deal of uncertainty and a fumbling on both sides for a satisfactory outcome.

A factor that makes for further uncertainty in the bargaining situation is the role of the Government as an employer. Since in many countries the Government is the major employer its decisions have a great impact on general wage levels and employment standards. As pointed out earlier, Governments were reluctant to grant bargaining rights to civil servants, but it gradually became obvious that it was impossible for a Government to give official support to the development of collective bargaining and not to practise what it preached with regard to its own employees. In Nigeria and in several other countries the Governments followed British practice and established joint councils — known as Whitley Councils — through which unions could participate in the determining of levels of wages and other conditions of service of employees.

The recognition of unions and the acceptance of a responsibility to consult and negotiate left the actual pay policy to be pursued unresolved. There have been inevitably different views as to whether the Government should lead or follow private enterprise in the setting of wage standards and other conditions of employment. Relations between Governments and private employers have on occasion been somewhat strained as a result of differing views as to the correct policy the Government should follow as an employer.

The problem of the appropriate role of the Government as an employer is certainly not confined to the English-speaking countries of Africa. It is one common to all states whether in Europe or Africa, whether industrially advanced or little developed, whether economic activity is primarily a function of the State or of private enterprise. The pressing concern of most Governments to secure a rapid rate of economic growth by encouraging investment, keeping consumption down and costs low, has led them to view the pressure of unions for higher pay as an activity endangering the achievement of these goals. On the other hand, unions have reflected the natural anxiety of their members to secure a higher standard of living. Whether these differing objectives can be reconciled without drastically curtailing the freedom of employers and unions to fix wages and conditions of employment by the bargaining process remains to be seen.

### The Settlement of Disputes Arising in the Process of Negotiations

In the various English-speaking countries of Africa the system of voluntary negotiation promoted under British direction has permitted a great deal of flexibility in the machinery developed for settling any disputes that might arise between unions and employers. Though the basic concepts in the early stages were the same, the procedures now reflect the most diverse notions as to the best methods, so to speak, of resolving conflicts. In most of these countries a faith in the advantages of free discussion and, on occasion, free confrontation of the opposing forces has made the settlement of disputes voluntary at every stage except in certain essential services. The Government offers the parties concerned its good offices. It may bring pressure to bear but there is no compulsory conciliation and either side is free to refuse. Only in the clearly defined cases of essential services is a dispute prevented by law from ending in a strike or lockout.[1] A minority of these countries — though an increasing number since they have attained independence — have found it necessary, while retaining the facilities for the free settlement of disputes, to supplement them on occasion with compulsory methods that are designed to prevent the resort to a trial of strength.

The first stage of official support to the negotiating system in all of the countries concerned is the provision of a conciliation service. In keeping with the 'liberal' approach conciliation is a function of the Labour Commissioner who generally has no power to intervene in negotiations unless asked to do so by one or both of the parties.

[1] At one period there was a tendency in Tanganyika and Kenya to extend the concept of essential service to cover a rather wide range of industries. Protest from the British TUC and the International Confederation of Free Trade Unions led to a reversal of this policy. See B. C. Roberts, *op. cit.*

In practice, however, the Commissioner or one of his officials will have been in close and continuous touch with both union leaders and employers on an informal basis and will be well aware of the problems to be overcome to bring the negotiations to a satisfactory conclusion. Both unions and employers have learned to look upon this type of discreet conciliation with confidence and to welcome the opportunity which it provides to get out of difficulties that would, without this type of third party assistance, have proved overwhelming. The achievement of the labour conciliation services has been outstanding. In Kenya, for instance, in 1962 very nearly nine-tenths of all disputes were settled at the conciliation stage.

When conciliation does fail, as it must on occasion, the dispute is referred, subject to the consent of both parties, to an Arbitration Tribunal, or, in some cases, a Commission of Inquiry is set up. An Arbitration Tribunal may consist of a sole arbitrator or of an arbitrator assisted by assessors nominated by the employers and the workers. The arbitrator may be a named person agreed upon by both employers and unions as, for example, is the case in the Tanzania sisal industry. Or the arbitrator might be drawn from an agreed panel of names and nominated by the Commissioner of Labour. Where the Tribunal consists of a group of persons it is usual for the Chairman to be appointed by the Commissioner or Minister of Labour.

An Arbitration Tribunal is usually an *ad hoc* body — though there may be a permanent arbitrator. But some countries — Southern Rhodesia in 1959 and Kenya more recently — have set up standing industrial courts with a view to ensuring greater uniformity and continuity in the awards made by arbitrators. These courts link judicial authority with the responsibilities of the Ministry of Labour. Permanent machinery for the settlement of disputes through a process of compulsory arbitration is still the exception. However, in recent years several countries, which have decided that they cannot allow industrial disputes to be resolved through the traditional processes of conciliation and voluntary arbitration, with its attendant risks of industrial stoppages, have set up such machinery. For example, the Labour Practices Review Board established in Liberia in 1961 ; the Labour Relations Board established in Ethiopia in 1962 ; and Tanzania has considered the setting up of a permanent Arbitration Tribunal to complement the 1962 amendment to the Trade Union Ordinance.

As in the French-speaking countries, this arbitration machinery is mainly a supplementary arrangement to be used only as a last resort. Following British procedure the laws generally seek to impose on the Minister of Labour the duty to make certain, before invoking his power to remit a dispute to arbitration, that the normal voluntary procedures established by the parties have clearly been exhausted. The object of this obligation is to discourage any tendency for the availability of arbitration procedures to undermine the duty of the parties to accept responsibility for arriving at their own settlements. However, experience has shown that when Government agencies are given the responsibility for making the final decision, after negotiation has failed to produce an agreement, there is a strong temptation, especially for weak unions, to prefer to rely upon this provision rather than upon their own strength. Thus, when compulsory arbitration is introduced, this often meets with the approval of unions which are not in a strong bargaining position.[1] Where, on the other hand, unions and employers have established a good relationship and both parties are confident that they will be able to arrive at constructive agreements, experience has also indicated, as previously pointed out in the case of Ghana, that voluntary settlement will remain important.

Arbitration is not restricted, as it is in the French-speaking countries, to the settlement of collective claims but in practice it has been mainly used for deciding issues of substance. There might be individual complaints as well as major claims. Since in the British tradition there is no clear distinction between disputes of rights and disputes of interests, there is also no special reason why a dispute of interpretation should be treated differently from one of substantial change. In the British system of industrial relations the appropriate method for smoothing out differences that arise out of the definition of the terms of an agreement is negotiation within the framework of the procedural agreement. This may involve, as a last resort, arbitration, but generally when a case is submitted to a Minister for reference to arbitration it involves a new element of substance as well as a pure question of interpretation.[2]

In addition to the conciliation and arbitration machinery, in most countries that follow the British tradition, the Government has a further legal means of acting during a dispute — even when the existence of the dispute is not yet officially recognised. This is the

---

[1] In this respect the response of unions in Africa is no different from unions in a weak bargaining position in Britain which have also welcomed compulsory arbitration. [2] On this subject, see Chapter 6.

appointment of a special court of inquiry having all the powers required to investigate the causes and circumstances of the dispute or the situation which threatens to lead to a strike or lockout. The Minister will normally publish the evidence received and the conclusions arrived at by the inquiry. It is this publicity and the appeal to public opinion that it implies that is expected to persuade the parties to accept voluntarily the findings of the inquiry as a satisfactory basis for an agreement. The report is not normally legally binding, but its moral authority is generally considerable and it is usually accepted as providing the basis for a settlement. The establishment of a court of inquiry, though not subject to the prior consent of the parties, is everywhere an exceptional step and in practice is only resorted to in situations that are particularly intractable and likely to give rise to serious trouble. It cannot, therefore, be regarded as a method that is in conflict with the general principles of free negotiation.

As a rule, awards are legally binding and in several countries, Uganda and Malawi, for example, a certain period of time must elapse before they may legally be reviewed. In fact, however, this procedure does not prevent a union from discovering an issue and submitting a claim which in effect involves a change in the prevailing conditions of employment.

The right to strike when an agreement cannot be reached on the terms and conditions of employment has been a basic assumption which the legal framework regulating collective bargaining in Britain has sought to sustain. In taking over this legal framework from Britain, the English-speaking countries of Africa have also accepted the assumption that the right to strike is an essential element in a collective bargaining system based upon the British model. Consequently, the launching of a strike was not in itself sufficient to start proceedings against a union under the criminal law or to bring civil action against a union or its members on the grounds of conspiracy to injure or inducement to break off a contract, or the causing of damage to property.

Nevertheless even in Britain, which has less legal regulation of its industrial relations than any other country in the world, there are certain legal limitations to the exercise of the right to strike. The police and the armed forces are not free to strike — though all other categories of civil servants as well as private employees enjoy the right to refuse to work on terms they do not approve. Strikes expressly to achieve political objectives rather than ends that are related in some sense to the terms and conditions of employment are probably not protected by the Trade Union and Trade Dispute Acts. The conduct of strikes is also limited by the law relating to intimidation and to unlawful assembly. These conditions apply in all the English-speaking African countries where it is usually the case that the law is rather more restrictively drawn than in Britain.

Under the Conspiracy and Protection of Property Act of 1875, a worker in Britain who 'wilfully and maliciously breaks a contract' in the knowledge that by stopping his work he risks endangering human life or the public well-being, or causes serious corporal injury or the destruction or loss of property, is guilty of an offence ; the laws of virtually all the English-speaking countries in Africa embody this provision. A union that abets a stoppage that would fall in this category would also be liable to prosecution in African countries, but not in Britain.

The most restrictive limitation on the right to strike in the English-speaking African countries is without question the law that applies to the 'essential services'. This restriction is based upon the British wartime essential services order, which sought to make unions and employers agree to submit any dispute to arbitration if they could not agree in private through the normal negotiating procedure. The principles of the order were extended to the colonial territories during the war period and with modification have tended to remain in force with amendments ever since. The main feature of this legislation is that unions are not permitted to strike or employers to lockout in the designated essential services — usually water, power and public health, including hospital services — without first exhausting their normal bargaining procedure and then reporting the deadlock to the Ministry of Labour. If the Minister or Commissioner fails to refer the dispute to arbitration within, say twenty-one days, the parties are free to take whatever action they choose including a stoppage of work. If the matter is remitted to arbitration then the parties must refrain from strikes or lockouts until an award has been made which is mandatory on both parties, but which in practice only really binds the employers, since in most cases it is possible to submit a fresh claim on the following day.

Ghana in 1958 and Tanzania in 1962 extended the system formerly applicable only to the designated essential services to all sectors of employment. Strikes and lockouts are now only allowed after the competent authorities have been notified that a dispute exists and a certain interval has elapsed without their taking steps to refer the dispute to arbitration. In Ghana a strike is always an offence when it involves workers who are not represented by a 'certificated' union. This means that certain groups of employees such as teachers and civil servants no longer have the right to strike under any circumstances. Moreover, the right to grant a certificate or to withdraw one from a union is entirely the prerogative of the Minister of Labour. Thus strong pressures can be brought to bear against unions that refuse to heed the official disapproval of the taking of strike action.

The Tanzanian Act of 1962, like the Ghanaian Act of 1958, makes arbitrators' awards subject to Government approval, and even explicitly empowers the Minister to refer unacceptable awards back to the tribunal and, if this does not produce a satisfactory amendment, to appoint another tribunal. None the less, the Act strongly stresses the obligation on the Labour Commissioner to explore at the very start the possibility of reaching an amicable settlement through the use of the machinery already in existence in the industry concerned, and if such machinery does not exist to take the steps necessary to ensure that it is set up.

Sudan and Ethiopia have both introduced laws that closely regulate industrial relations and strictly curtail strike activities. The Minister in both cases may refer a dispute to an arbitration tribunal on his own initiative, without the consent of the parties, whenever he considers this to be an expedient step, and awards are binding. Strikes started before negotiations begin or while settlement procedure is in progress are outlawed, as are those that infringe any agreement in force or transgress an arbitration award.

In Kenya, joint action by the Department of Labour and the National Organisation of Workers and Employers, has produced a stable system of industrial relations based upon the principles of voluntary negotiation introduced by the Colonial Government. In spite of the fact that an adequate system of industrial relations seemed to have been established, the right to strike has been further limited by an Act of June 1965. The restrictions imposed do not, however, substitute compulsory arbitration for the free agreement of the parties ; they merely oblige the latter to resort to machinery for voluntary negotiation and settlement, if it exists, and to respect agreements and awards already in force. Where no such machinery, agreements or awards in a given enterprise or industry exist, the Minister has no power to declare illegal a strike in support of a claim by workers or their union. Strikes which have no connection with a trade dispute and sympathetic strikes have been also made illegal.

In this respect Kenya has borrowed from the British 1927 Trade Unions and Trade Disputes Act which made sympathetic strikes, and strikes designed to coerce the Government, illegal. Strikes unrelated to disputes about the terms and conditions of employment are also illegal under the legislation in force in the Sudan and Ethiopia.

In the English-speaking countries of Africa, and others such as the Sudan and Ethiopia, there has been in recent years a shift away from the traditional British principles of industrial relations to methods involving more legal regulation ; but in spite of this development there remains a strong attachment to voluntary negotiation and settlement. It is true that the limitations on the right to strike have not aroused the hostility of the unions that might have been expected. This in part is because not all awards have been favourable to the employers and arbitrators have sometimes fixed wages at levels that it would have been hard for the unions to obtain, given the relative strength of the parties by free bargaining and even strike action.[1] Moreover, many union leaders are thankful to be relieved of the responsibility of calling for strike action which might well end in disaster. However, it would be foolish not to recognise the existence of a strong sentiment in Africa for centralised authoritarian methods of government and its influence on labour relations systems. Strikes not only threaten economic and political stability, but they imply a social criticism of the policies being pursued by the government. It is understandable that African leaders, who are the fathers of their nations, should resent this manifestation of independence and seek to protect themselves and the public from its consequences.

There can be no doubt that the restrictions on strike action have strong support from most Africans holding official positions in Government and the trade unions ; but there are those who have reservations about these limitations, and the outbreaks of opposition that have occurred have demonstrated that public tolerance of the restriction could change if the policy was pressed too hard. It is important not to over-estimate the differences that exist between the various English-speaking African countries in this respect. In fact in those countries that have officially banned strikes, there is a widespread recognition of the advantage of arriving at voluntary settlements. It is difficult to say exactly where the balance will eventually

[1] This was particularly apparent in Tanzania in the period following the adoption of compulsory arbitration, and explains that the reform was welcomed by practically all the unions (except the big plantation workers' union) while the employers' reactions were in general much less favourable.

be struck between the collective bargaining system established during the period of development under British colonial rule, and a more closely regulated and centrally administered system of industrial relations. Much will depend upon the political and economic development of the countries of Africa and the extent to which they can achieve social stability. When we come to consider the situation in the French-speaking countries, we see at once that collective bargaining has occupied a different place in the system of industrial relations.

## II. COLLECTIVE BARGAINING IN THE FRENCH-SPEAKING COUNTRIES

### Collective Bargaining and the Labour Code of 1952

A brief description of the fundamental elements in the system of industrial relations introduced with the promulgation, in 1952, of the *Code du Travail des Territoires d'Outre-Mer* (Labour Code for overseas territories), will give an idea of the legal framework regulating labour matters in the French-speaking countries of Africa today. There have been some changes in certain countries, but the *Code* of 1952 remains in force in several of them. In the countries where the *Code* of 1952 has been replaced by a new Code, the new provisions are either for the most part taken over from the old text or take their inspiration from it on numerous points. Notable innovations have been introduced in certain cases.

When the *Code du Travail* for overseas territories was in the process of discussion, there was considerable debate between the advocates of a liberal approach to collective bargaining and those who favoured a strict control of collective agreements, which under the law might become legally binding on all employers in the sector covered. The controversy was settled in favour of permitting the parties to a collective agreement freely to discuss and settle its terms without the need to have them formally approved by the Government, which had been required under previous legislation. In this respect the French National Assembly followed the wishes of the deputies from the territories concerned and decided to apply the same principle of freedom of discussion of the terms of collective agreements to the overseas territories as was permitted in Metropolitan France under the law on collective bargaining passed in 1950. However, in the event the law produced somewhat different results.

This was in part due to amendments made necessary by a need to take into account certain local conditions and by a reluctance in practice to leave the settlement of agreements to an autonomous dialogue between the parties. The result has been to make collective bargaining as close to an administrative process as to a free negotiation.

Parallel to the ordinary collective agreement, which is subject to no particular limitations as to its form, its field of application or its contents — as long as it does not contravene statutory conditions and does not include clauses less favourable to the workers it covers than those provided for by law and other regulation — the *Code* sets up a special category of agreements, the so-called 'extendable agreements'. These agreements, which may be made applicable to a wider body of workers than those represented in the actual negotiations, are subject to a series of provisions which in certain respects limit the freedom of the parties, while giving the State ample opportunity for intervention in the negotiating process. Since in practice this type of agreement is very frequently adopted, the autonomous bargaining which the drafters of the legislation had initially sought to encourage, has never been extensively carried out.

The capacity to negotiate an 'extendable' agreement is reserved to the organisations of workers and employers considered by the Government to be most representative. In deciding whether a given organisation is representative or not, the administrative authority is entitled to consider the extent of a union's membership, the financial status and extent to which contributions have been paid, its past experience, its type of activities and, finally its independence from external control ; the *Code*, however, does not give the administration the power to examine the membership registers and the financial records of the union, and an appeal against the decision of the administrative officer concerned may be made to the Minister responsible.

Negotiations do not consist merely of dialogue between the representative of the unions and employers ; they have to be conducted within a joint commission made up of equal numbers of workers and employer representatives ; the composition of this commission is prescribed by an order of the competent minister. The fact that a collective agreement is thus the product of a collective body with an official status, as previous studies have pointed out,[1] gives the agreement more of the character of an administrative regulation than a bilateral bargain.

[1] Gonidek and Kirsch, *Droit du travail des territoires d'outre-mer*, p. 143.

This administrative aspect of the bargaining process under the *Code du Travail* of 1952 is accentuated by the fact that these agreements cover a whole section of economic activity, such as transport or commerce, and within that section all occupations and occupational categories such as engineers, supervisors, clerical and manual workers. Provision has been made, however, for the specific needs of the various occupational categories and also the particular situation existing in a limited geographical area. Features of employment peculiar to the different categories may be negotiated separately by their representatives and included in annexes to the main agreement. The agreements can be concluded at the regional, or local level as well as at the federal or territorial (today at the national) level. Where a federal, territorial or national agreement exists, it may be supplemented by sub-agreements that reflect local conditions,[1] and, whatever the territorial scope of an industry-wide agreement, its provisions may be made more specific at the plant level with regard to such matters as payment-by-results schemes.

With reference to the negotiating process itself, the *Code* states, 'If a joint committee is unable to overcome a difference of opinion regarding one or more provisions to be inserted in the collective agreement, the Inspectorate of Labour shall, at the request of any of the parties, assist in overcoming such disagreement'. In practice the committees work under the guidance of a high civil servant of the Ministry of Labour, usually a director of labour or an inspector-general who is able to exercise an important influence on the outcome of the discussions. In this respect the role of this official might seem to be similar to that exercised by the chairman of a wages council in the United Kingdom or Sierra Leone. There is an important difference, however, that arises from the status of the administrative authority under the *Code du Travail*. In the British case the chairman is rarely if ever an employee of the State and his role is seen as that of an impartial president whose prime function is to help the parties to find an acceptable solution. Thus, a collective agreement in the British system does not owe its validity to the law, but to the labour market — when the terms are given legal validity the process by which they are arrived at fundamentally remains unchanged.

Once a collective agreement has been reached under the *Code du Travail* by the means outlined, the administrative authorities, either

[1] Thus, in the old Federations, wages were negotiated at the level of each territory, the federal agreement being confined to a statement of the general principles to be followed in the matter.

70

on the request of a representative union or on their own initiative can extend the agreement — that is to say give the agreement the force of law for all employers and employees in its occupational and territorial field of application, whether or not they were represented at the original negotiations. Such a decision must be preceded by consultation with the organisations and persons concerned, who are given a time limit of thirty days for the submission of comments, but none the less the decision is still of a discretionary nature. Moreover, when an agreement is extended, the authorities exercise a control, which, it has been said, gives them the appearance of being to an important degree the 'co-authors' of the agreement ; thus an agreement ceases to be the exclusive product of the joint negotiations between the unions and employers but is instead 'the common work of the group and the administration'.[1] Apart from having the duty to exclude, from the agreement to be extended, those provisions which are in contradiction to existing laws and regulations, the authorities can more arbitrarily omit from the agreement at their discretion, so long as they do not alter its basic features, 'any clauses which are inappropriate to the situation in the branch of activity in the area under consideration'.[2]

All collective agreements which are extended, or any subsequent modifications, must be published in the official gazette ; this procedure again tends to give them the character of an administrative order.

Thus the normal legal process of concluding collective agreements offers the administration ample means to ensure that those considerations it may deem important should be given due weight even if they cannot be given an absolute priority. This appears even more clearly when the use to which the procedure has been put is studied.

The procedure for settling collective disputes in the *Code* for overseas territories of 1952, as amended in 1955, includes three stages : [3] (1) conciliation by a Labour Inspector ; (2) mediation by an independent expert (who must not be a civil servant or a person directly concerned in the dispute) ; and (3) arbitration by an 'arbitration tribunal' composed of a magistrate and two independent assessors. At each of these stages the parties must accept the third party under

[1] Gonidek and Kirsch, *op. cit.* p. 142.
[2] *Code du Travail*, Article 76.
[3] Not including the final appeal to the Supreme Court in the former metropolitan country, which could only be made on the grounds of action that was *ultra vires* or contrary to the law at a previous stage of the procedure. An appeal could only result in the case being handed over to a new expert or a new arbitration tribunal.

threat of penal sanction. But, as with a conciliation agreement, the 'recommendation' of the mediator or the decision of the arbitration tribunal becomes mandatory only with consent of both parties who are given a few days in which to express any opposition. Whilst the authors of the *Code* wanted to ensure as far as possible that a settlement of a dispute would be achieved without a strike, they also felt obliged to preserve the right to strike, since this right is guaranteed by the French constitution, thus they had to allow the parties the opportunity of refusing to accept the outcome of the appeal to the expert or the tribunal.[1]

Once the means of conciliation have been exhausted, the strike or lockout is considered legal and no penalty is incurred. Nor does a stoppage constitute a breach of contract of employment (unless there is 'grievous fault' by a worker), entitling the employer lawfully to dismiss an employee. Only those strikes and lockouts started before the peaceful means of settlement have been exhausted, or in violation of the provisions of an agreement, a recommendation or a decision that have acquired executory force, are liable to sanctions. These sanctions are, however, of a purely civil or administrative kind and are not penal. For the worker they may involve instant dismissal. For the employer they may involve payment of wages to the workers for the days lost because of the lockout, ineligibility to hold certain positions and the disallowing of the right to conclude contracts with a public authority.

The *Code* (Art. 74) also allows the parties to an agreement to provide arbitration machinery for themselves to deal with any dispute which may arise after the conclusion of the agreement. Where such machinery exists the procedure to be followed is that laid down in the agreement, but this procedure is usually limited to the settlement of disputes arising out of the application or interpretation of the agreement; it would not cover disputes arising from the modification or renewal of the agreement which would be dealt with under the other provisions of the *Code*.

The *Code* borrows from the French law of December 1946 to lay down that in the absence of, or pending the conclusion of, a collective agreement, the administration authorities can replace the parties and on its own initiative regulate the conditions of employment in a given occupation 'by following the general lines of any other collective

---

[1] In France arbitration awards are binding but the free exercise of the right to strike is assured by allowing the parties a free choice as to whether they will agree to the matter being referred to arbitration.

agreements which may exist in the French Union'. This provision was designed not so much to permit the Government to settle the conditions of employment arbitrarily, as to give it power to exert pressure when one or the other of the parties appeared disinclined to arrive at a reasonable compromise.

## The Legislative Evolution since Independence

The *Code du Travail* of 1952, with its subsequent modifications, is still in force today in the following French-speaking countries : Chad, Cameroon, Togo and Dahomey. In some of these a new Code is being prepared.[1]

In most French-speaking countries where, since independence, legislative reform has passed the planning stage, more or less similar roads have been followed. The new Codes, whilst they reveal certain differences, have many points in common, and in certain aspects only do they depart from the 1952 *Code*.

In general, the rules on the commencement and conduct of collective bargaining — before the stage of a dispute is reached — have been retained more or less unchanged. From this it can be concluded that since 1952 the principles involved have satisfied employers' organisations and workers' unions as well as the authorities. The distinction between ordinary collective agreements and those which are capable of extension has been retained everywhere. Also retained has been the system of establishing a negotiating group consisting of the most representative unions or organisations, which can be called into being at the compulsory request of one of the parties or the Government. Most of the details of procedure have been borrowed literally from the 1952 *Code*.[2] It is interesting to note that all the new Codes apart from those of Upper Volta, Guinea and Congo (Brazzaville) insist that agreements must be drafted in French.

Those changes that have taken place nearly all tend to strengthen the powers of government. For example it has been thought desirable, by several countries, to give the administrative authorities

---

[1] In Cameroon the promulgation of a new Code is hampered by a barrier that is difficult to overcome. In theory labour legislation is the responsibility of the Federation, but in fact there are two quite distinct systems in the eastern and western parts and their unification is made difficult by the inequality of economic and social development.

[2] Some changes have been made necessary by constitutional developments. In the Ivory Coast and the Republic of Madagascar the procedure for conducting agreements is not described in detail by the Code, since it has been left to special decrees.

greater freedom to evaluate the representative character of trade unions. This has led Gabon and the Republic of Madagascar to eliminate the criteria which were laid down in the *Code* of 1952. Elsewhere, these criteria have been retained, but in Mali, Guinea and Congo (Brazzaville) the Government may now take into account the results of elections for *délégués du personnel* before accepting a union as a representative body for bargaining purposes. The possibility of an appeal against a decision of the Minister of Labour, except in the case of Mali and the Republic of Madagascar, is still expressly mentioned. This is usually to the President of the Republic or the Prime Minister ; in Guinea, an appeal must be made to the administrative tribunals ; in Gabon it is limited to a request for a fresh examination by the Minister. In Gabon and Mali the Government is no longer limited in the control that it might exercise over union finance and membership as it was under the 1952 *Code*. The truth of the matter is that the whole question of representativeness is losing most of its practical importance as the trade union movements are unified and increasingly brought under government control in the French-speaking countries of Africa.

The rules relating to the conduct of bargaining itself have not been changed very much. The legislatures in Niger, Upper Volta and Mali, have found it useful to make clear that joint committees set up for the purpose of establishing agreements are to be presided over by the Minister of Labour or his representative — often the Chief Labour Inspector. This, however, has always been normal practice. In Gabon, the law now specifically indicates that bargaining can be carried on simultaneously between several trade unions and employers' organisations for the purpose of concluding an agreement that will cover a number of occupations. The Code in Guinea provides that should international agreements be in existence they shall have the same relation to agreements at the national level as do national agreements to local agreements. In other words they may only be applied on the territory of the Republic of Guinea in a way which is more favourable to the workers involved.

The procedure for extending collective agreements, which generally remains the same as that set up by the *Code* of 1952, has been modified in Senegal and Niger so as to make it more speedy and also to strengthen the powers of the Minister. In the case of wages an extension can be decided upon without any preliminary consultation with the organisations and persons concerned (who in other fields retain their right to submit comments within thirty days). This innovation has been introduced in an attempt to avoid delays in the equalising of levels of pay in those establishments covered by the union signing the agreement and those that were outside. In this regard the Gabon has adopted a policy that is still more radical, since an agreement may now be extended without any consultation with the interested parties. The act of extension in Senegal and Mauritania, is significantly the result of a joint decree by the Minister of Labour and the Minister of Finance.

The administration in all countries (except the Ivory Coast) has kept the power, in the absence of new collective agreements, to determine conditions of employment by means of regulations. However, those regulations must not henceforth take their inspiration from the other agreements of the French Union, but as the case may be, from the 'agreements in force' (Niger, Central African Republic, Gabon, Uppa Volta), or the 'agreements existing in other states or internationally recognised standards' (Senegal and Mauritania). The Code of Guinea refers to 'the most favourable agreements existing in other countries', whilst in Mali the Code omits all references which could conceivably limit the administration's freedom of action.

Thus until now no substantial modifications have been made in the normal procedure for concluding collective agreements. Only in Mali has the necessity of obtaining the approval of the Government been made concrete, though this has been normal practice for a long time to varying degrees in most of the countries.[1]

However, the situation is rather different in the case of disputes that might arise in the course of negotiating a new or modifying an old agreement. The procedures in this respect have undergone in most cases a major modification. The right of the parties to refuse to accept an arbitrated award has been maintained in Niger, Madagascar, the Central African Republic, Congo (Brazzaville) and even, quite surprisingly, in Guinea, but measures allowing the Minister to have disputes settled by arbitration — without any right of appeal other than on the grounds of *ultra vires* — when he feels that a strike or lockout would prejudice public order and be contrary to the general interest — have been adopted by Gabon, Mali, Senegal, the Ivory Coast, the Upper Volta and Mauritania. The arbitration tribunals established under these circumstances are generally presided over by a magistrate and, in some cases (Mali, the Central

[1] The drafting of the new law does not make it clear whether the powers conferred upon the Minister go beyond a simple supervision of the legality of the agreement.

African Republic and the Gabon for example) include also a civil servant from the Ministry of Labour and representatives of the employers and the workers. However, none of the new Codes, except for Mali's, make this procedure compulsory unless there is no other machinery for the settlement of disputes, or that machinery has been tried and failed. The new Codes have not increased the sanctions that already existed against illegal strikes.

An effort has been made to speed up the process of hearing a dispute and the making of an award or decision. Except in Senegal, Upper Volta and Mauritania, any intermediate stage between conciliation and the final hearing has been eliminated. In Senegal and Upper Volta 'mediation' by an independent expert no longer exists as it did under the old *Code* of 1952, but the arbitration stage has been divided into two ; thus the difference is small. In the Ivory Coast mediation and arbitration are quite separate courses between which the parties can choose.

*Theory and Practice*

The modifications to the *Code* of 1952 have been made to harmonise with the wider role of the state in economic and social affairs. State intervention in the bargaining process tends to be more and more a customary feature in countries that are anxious to prevent any private interference with the achievement of the goals of public policy.

The practical consequences of the legal reform must, however, not be overestimated. It has generally not been the cause, but rather the consequence of changes in social patterns of behaviour. These changes have taken place everywhere, though they have not always been reflected in changes in the law.

The role of the administration has been closely related to the weakness of the trade unions in the past. Where unions were strong the State was not required to prop up their organisation and bargaining power. In the period before unions were effectively consolidated the State was inevitably called upon to redress the balance. The Labour Inspectorate grew to its modern significance under these conditions. These officials were in the French tradition closely connected with the administration of a centrally concerned and uniformly administered labour policy. This explains why in the French-speaking countries, even now, collective agreements have a good deal in common from Nouakchott to Brazzaville and from

Dakar to Bangui. The wage scales which complemented those agreements were diversified according to the territory, but unions seem to have been unable to make any major change in the level of the minimum wage as determined by Government order. The legal minimum (SMIG) tended to become also a legal maximum for the majority of workers. However, whilst having little aggregate effect, the unions were not totally deprived of influence.

These basic features appear to have been accentuated in all the countries under review since independence was granted to them. Everywhere, whatever be the pattern of legislation introduced, or the political philosophy of the State, the recasting of the old agreements is in the first place a Government concern. It is not only in Guinea or Mali that a high official of the Ministry of Labour might go so far as to pose as the architect, if not the author of collective agreements.

It must not be deduced from this general pattern of industrial relations that, within the joint committees, employers' and workers' representatives are more passive today than they were in the past. Although the administration is often the dominant influence neither employers nor workers are lacking negotiators who are able and willing to put forward a strongly argued case. Several examples might be given, from recent agreements (particularly in Senegal and Cameroon) in which in the course of their adoption significant changes were secured as a result of the advocacy of the workers' representatives. In one case that might be cited, considerable improvements in holidays and seniority provisions were secured following persistent efforts on behalf of the employees by their representatives. It sometimes happens that the basis of the discussion is a draft proposal from the unions or employers with the administration remaining content to exercise a discreet influence rather than play a relatively dominant role. Moreover, job classification is still a matter which arouses prolonged and effective discussion at the enterprise level.

However, while the representatives of the workers may still play a relatively effective part in the settlement of the non-wage elements, their influence on the general level of wages has been greatly reduced and in some cases it might be said almost eliminated. The Governments of most of the French-speaking countries are extremely reluctant to permit union pressure for higher wages to imperil a precarious economic stability. Since they are often the most important employers themselves, if wages rise this is at the cost of their exiguous revenues. This explains why official bargaining on wages is almost

77

at a standstill today. Where wage increases have been negotiated (for example, in Cameroon), the figures finally adopted were very close to the employers' original offer. These increases, in fact, represented no more than the minimum compensation for the rise in the cost of living that had occurred. They had been decided upon in the first instance as appropriate by the employers, with the tacit consent of the Government which was highly concerned as an employer itself. Adjustments in the level of pay have been frequently made outside the negotiating procedure when required by change in the cost of living, which under existing conditions is the main determinant, by a reclassification of the personnel grades and by the granting of *ad hoc* bonus awards. Thus wage changes are to a considerable extent determined unilaterally by the employers, closely following the attitude adopted by the Government.[1]

Where collective disputes are concerned the changes introduced by the new codes in the majority of the countries, as previously pointed out, are much more substantial than changes in the methods of negotiation. But when the new situation is examined closely there seems to be a much greater appearance of change than has actually occurred. It is doubtful, in particular, whether arbitration is more significant since the adoption of the new codes than under the earlier regulations. In fact there is some reason to believe that the opposite might well be true.

Even under the previous dispute settlement procedure, which in all the territories consisted of a three-stage mechanism for voluntary conciliation, mediation and arbitration, many disputes were settled informally before any resort to this machinery was made. For the rest, the great majority of disputes were settled at the conciliation stage. Where a labour inspector had failed in his efforts to bring the parties to an amicable agreement, the mediator or arbitrator only rarely succeeded in achieving a settlement.

Nevertheless it could be said that the awards of arbitrators in

---

[1] An example from Togo illustrates the present pattern of wage determination. In October 1963, the Togo Government, feeling that the blocking of wages which had gone on for several years could not any longer be maintained because of the rise in prices which had occurred, decided to raise the wages of its officials to the limit it believed the budgetary situation would permit, namely 5 per cent. At the same time private employers were invited to consent to an appropriate increase for their own employees. In the event the employers were prepared to be quite liberal and they let the Government know that the possible margin of increase would be at least 10 per cent. The Government, concerned to avoid too great a disparity between its own pay levels and rate of increase, asked the private employers to limit the rise they were prepared to make to a maximum of 8 per cent. On this basis wages were increased without the unions being called upon to play any role at all.

certain important cases had a significant effect. Today few disputes are allowed to reach the point of deadlock where an arbitrated award is the only solution. The combination of persuasion and pressure which is applied on unions from within as well as from without, together with the obvious limitations of the economic situation, almost always ensure that a dispute will not break out into open conflict. Although in theory arbitration is now given greater emphasis, neither employers nor unions have become more inclined to use this method of settling their differences. In difficult cases discussions will be drawn out as long as necessary to persuade union negotiators to accept the view of the authorities as to what a reasonable settlement ought to be. Even when this means that the union must abandon most of its claims a trial of strength is unlikely since, even if strong enough to strike, this would bring the unions into an overt conflict with the Government. Knowing that they are not likely to secure from an arbitration a better final decision, unions show little enthusiasm for carrying their struggle to this point. Employers, likewise, can see little advantage in allowing a final decision to be made by an outsider when they and the Government share a common interest in keeping pay increases down to a modest level. Whilst in the past decade there have been a number of strikes in these countries over conditions of employment, today the strike has been almost completely set aside as a method of securing pay increases. Most of the industrial stoppages that occur do so spontaneously and they are generally an immediate demonstration of protest against some unpopular decision of management. In this context the fact that arbitration is compulsory means relatively little, since as a settlement procedure it has lost most of its *raison d'être*.

Consequently the machinery set up under several of the new codes has had little opportunity to be tested, least of all in countries such as Mali where the changes in labour conditions presuppose, more than elsewhere, the agreement of the Government, if not its initiative. Conversely, in Guinea, the lack in the new Code of any formal procedure for compulsory arbitration has not resulted in a different pattern of behaviour. Moreover, the provision for compulsory arbitration in the Senegalese Code has not proved to be incompatible with an official policy which leaves more room for real bargaining between employers and unions — nor again is the total behaviour pattern very different from that observed in the other French-speaking countries of Africa.

To the contrary of what a simple survey of the alterations in the

*Code du Travail* might suggest, the general framework of the dialogue between workers and employers over the settlement of their conditions of employment has undergone a deeper transformation than the methods used for settling disputes. However, if the Government plays a more obviously dominant role, it is not one that totally ignores the pressures that are generated by social and economic forces and are expressed through unions and employers. The changes in the formal institutions are real, but they only imperfectly measure the actual process of adjustment that inevitably has had to take place. Whether the present or the past system is properly described as collective bargaining depends upon the definition employed. In any case, in the French-speaking countries the process is much closer to that of administrative decision-making than that of a bargain between independent agents in a market free from all but the minimum of non-economic restraints.[1]

[1] As an illustration of the legal approach to industrial relations which is found in the French-speaking countries, the sections of the Senegalese Labour Code that relate to collective agreements and disputes are reproduced in Annex II, following the 1962 Kenyan Industrial Charter (Annex 1) which offers a typical example of industrial self-regulation.

Chapter 5

# THE CONTENT OF COLLECTIVE AGREEMENTS

THE diversity of the methods and procedures of collective bargaining examined in the previous chapter are reflected in the form and content of the agreements that are adopted. In the French-speaking countries, where the collective agreement is the outcome of a discussion within a corporate body in which the representative of the public authorities occupies a paramount position, the agreement has all the features of a workers' charter for the employees in the section of employment covered. In this respect it is interesting to note that this is how agreements were first defined by legal commentators. A major agreement made in the French-speaking countries covers virtually every aspect of the relations between employers and employed, and even mentions, side by side with the clauses drafted jointly by the parties, the provisions of the law to which the signatories want to draw the attention of all concerned.[1] Since the agreements in the French-speaking countries have a common origin, they greatly resemble each other in their general pattern and even in their wording. The common character of these agreements was enhanced by the fact that they were adopted originally under the aegis of the two former great federations of West and Central Africa. Wage agreements alone were peculiar to each territory.

In the English-speaking countries they have differed more widely since they have not been produced from a common mould. Their scope and range has varied with the whims and desires of the bargaining parties rather than with the need to meet the requirements of a previously adopted labour code. In the English-speaking countries collective agreements are often briefer and more limited in their purpose. They frequently simply embody the results of a discussion between employers and unions on a limited number of well-defined points. Although some agreements may be all-inclusive and cover the whole span of employment issues, many are focussed simply on

[1] The various Labour Codes in force contain a list of subject-matters that *must* be dealt with in every 'extendable' agreement (see Annex II).

procedural questions or on a limited number of substantive issues such as wages and hours of work. Consequently, it is not uncommon to find that, even where the matters arising out of relations between employers and workers have been defined in all their essential aspects, they are set out not in a single, more or less comprehensive document, but in a series of fragmentary agreements, which may have been concluded at widely differing dates. For example, there may well be separate agreements covering the recognition of a union, procedural questions concerned with the making, amending and enforcement of agreements and such matters as wages or other conditions of employment. As pointed out in the previous chapter, there is much informal discussion and conventional procedure in the collective bargaining system followed in the English-speaking countries. A change in working conditions or the granting of an important concession, after a discussion between union representatives and employers, may often be simply given effect in a managerial order issued by the employer rather than incorporated in a formal, written bilateral agreement. In some cases the minutes of a meeting of a joint committee, at which one or more issues were dealt with to the greater or lesser satisfaction of the two parties, take the place of separate documents. In certain cases, where agreements cover an entire industry, the contents are all-inclusive and under the law are binding upon the parties ; they very closely resemble a code of law. Negotiations undertaken within the framework of a Joint Industrial Council, even when they concern a large sector of the economy, or between an employers' federation and a federation of unions, may confine themselves to establishing general principles or minimum conditions of employment, leaving to further negotiation at local level the settlement of terms relating to specific groups of employees.[1] Thus, under the theory and practice of collective bargaining in the English-speaking countries, there is a wide diversity of method and substantive results. And this remains despite the unifying influence inevitably exerted by the evolution of standardised procedures and greater centralisation of policy-making under social and economic pressures.

This greater diversity of form and content makes the systematic study of collective agreements a more complex problem in the English-speaking countries of Africa than in the French-speaking ones. However, it is possible to make a uniform classification of the content of collective agreements that is applicable to all countries.

[1] For example, in the plantation industry of Nigeria.

The subject-matter covered in collective agreements may be divided into two major categories, the procedural and the substantive. The provisions relating to the first category cover the making, amending and enforcement of a collective agreement ; in the second category the provisions of the agreement relate to the specific standards of wages and other working conditions which make up the actual terms and conditions of employment. In this chapter procedural items will be touched upon only in so far as they are related to the substantive provisions. In so far as procedural matters have not been already dealt with in the previous chapter they will be treated in Chapter 6.

The provisions covering the substantive conditions of employment include in the first instance the terms on which a union will be recognised for bargaining purposes, union security provisions, including the check-off, the right of access to members and the extent to which exclusive bargaining rights will be granted.

## THE EXERCISE OF TRADE UNION RIGHTS

Virtually all major agreements contain provisions relating to trade union rights. The interpretation of these rights reflects the different systems of industrial relations and reveals the different attitudes which prevail towards the vital problems that arise out of their exercise.

In the agreements concluded in the French-speaking countries, the principle of freedom of association is stated in its most general — one might almost say its abstract — form. The contracting parties formally recognise the right of all workers to associate and act freely in the collective defence of their occupational interests. Employers agree not to take into account, when hiring an employee, allocating jobs, making a change in work organisation, applying disciplinary measures, making dismissals or promotions, the fact that a worker is or is not a member of a trade union and does or does not engage in union activities. They also undertake not to bring any pressure to bear on workers to join one union or another. In sum, the basic rule followed by employers is absolute non-interference in internal union affairs. In their turn, unions agree not to seek to coerce workers who hold different opinions about union policy into changing their mind, or to seek to prevent them joining another union, or to question their refusal to belong to any union at all. Thus, both sides interpret freedom of association in terms of the rights of the individual to choose to join a union and to act accordingly without constraint.

In the English-speaking countries which have adopted British theory and practice, the commitment to the abstract principle is regarded in a different light. The interest of the individual worker is considered to be more effectively advanced if his rights are to some degree subordinated to the need to provide for a genuine system of representation and by ensuring its consistency and stability to build up the strengths of the organisation. Instead of solemn declarations of fundamental rights, agreements usually contain concrete provisions, giving explicit and sometimes exclusive recognition to the contracting union as the representative organisation of the workers concerned. This specific recognition considerably strengthens the union's authority over its members, especially since the employer's undertaking not to recognise any other union or rival group that might be formed by members of the enterprise while the agreement is in force, is further supported by registration provisions which limit the right of new unions to secure the legal permission to exist when there is already an established organisation in being.

The security of a recognised union is further enhanced when an employer agrees to make an automatic deduction of union contributions from the worker's pay packet (check-off) on its behalf. However, it is normal for such a deduction to be made only after a wage earner has given his consent in writing which is revocable at any time. In the French-speaking countries the check-off system is banned as it presents at least a threat to the independence of the union and the freedom of the individual. The check-off has found few supporters in Britain for the same reasons, and British unions with few exceptions have preferred to collect their own contributions, but in the United States the check-off became a feature of the revival of trade union organisations during the 'New Deal' period. The unions in the English-speaking countries in Africa have adopted the check-off because they have recognised, as did the unions in America, that it offers practical advantages to weak organisations. At first there was opposition from employers and no support from the authorities; however, this hostility has gradually given way to approval.[1] As a rule the employers give their services free of charge or for a low charge. In Ghana, Tanzania and Kenya the union may compel

---

[1] One practical reason why employers have favoured the check-off is that it does away with the pestering of workers for union contributions immediately after they have been paid and the need for a clause such as the one in a Uganda agreement forbidding the collection of contributions less than fifty yards from the pay Office.

employers to agree to a check-off by law.[1]

The more radical method of giving the unions security, namely the making of union membership a condition of employment, which is commonplace in the U.S.A., has not been adopted as a general feature of the industrial relations systems in the English-speaking countries of Africa, with the exception of Ghana and Tanzania, where it is provided for by legal regulation. An agreement concluded during the war covering skilled workers in the Zambian copper mines appears to be one of the few examples of a 'closed shop' agreement that has been voluntarily adopted. This particular agreement would probably not have been conceded by the employers had not the situation especially favoured the union. On the other hand, a great many agreements are in accord with those in French-speaking countries, in explicitly banning all discrimination by the employer against union members as well as intimidation or pressure by the union on non-members. In some countries legislation was passed whilst under British rule making any kind of discrimination by employers against union membership illegal. Where this was the case compulsory union membership could not be enforced since it would involve the employer in a violation of the law.

The recognition granted to a union by voluntary agreement is often subject to the condition that a certain minimum proportion — usually 40 or 50 per cent — of the workers in the enterprise or industry in question must have joined the union. In the absence of a check-off it is normally accepted that an employer has the right to demand proof of membership before agreeing to bargain with the union. This demand can be justified especially if there are rival claims for recognition. There is a substantial justification for a clause in an agreement that entitles an employer to withdraw recognition from a union if he is notified by his workers that they no longer consider that this organisation represents their interests. If his assertion is subsequently checked by a secret ballot, as is provided for in at least one agreement [2] then there is an overwhelming case, from the angle of trade union democracy, against continuance of the exclusive recognition of the union which has lost support.

Quite a number of agreements stipulate that recognition may be questioned, not only if membership of the union falls below an agreed figure, but also if the union acts in breach of its rules or so

---

[1] Although employers may be compelled to deduct contributions, the individual worker is still entitled to refuse his consent to this measure.
[2] In the Total Oil Company agreement in Nigeria.

changes them as to alter the basis on which the employer originally agreed to the recognition. In Uganda, where there was an attempt to get rid of unions controlled from outside the country, employers granted recognition on condition that the union did not affiliate to a blanket organisation controlled or influenced from another country.[1] In other cases the check-off has been subject to the union refraining from engaging in political activity.[2] Some agreements stipulate that the union must submit its books to the scrutiny of the employer from time to time. In a number of cases in Zambia the union is under an obligation to submit its books at regular intervals to the management or to an accountant approved by management. However, clauses of this kind, which, it could be argued, are violations of the principle of non-intervention in the affairs of the union, do not give the employer any real financial control over union affairs. Some agreements in fact actually state that the administration of a check-off scheme does not give the employer any right to interfere in the financial affairs of the union.

The right of unions to have access to employees on company premises was, in the early days of trade union development, often vigorously contested by employers. Nowadays it is quite common for the conditions under which access is permitted to a union officer to be laid down in a collective agreement. These usually entail a union giving notice, in advance, to management of the intention of its representative to visit its members in the enterprise.

The activities of the union in the plant, such as holding meetings on the premises of the employer, or the posting of notices, are now generally permitted under defined conditions which normally include the agreement of the employer. It is often laid down that meetings on company premises shall take place after working hours ; that they must be conducted in an orderly manner and not give rise to any damage to the property of the undertaking. Communication from the union must be confined to matters related to the occupational interests of the members. In all this the pattern of behaviour and conventions that have been established in the larger enterprises in the English-speaking African countries bear comparison with those that exist in the more advanced industrial countries. They seem to hold a reasonable balance between the interest of the employer not to have the daily work routine disturbed and the necessary require-

---

[1] Several Uganda agreements contain clauses of this kind.
[2] In a Malawi plantations' agreement it is specifically stated that association with a political party would not be a breach of the principles embodied in the agreement.

ments of the union to have reasonable opportunity to maintain contact with its members. There are, of course, employers who are more strict in their interpretation of these needs than others, but in this respect there is no fundamental difference between the African countries and elsewhere.

A problem which can give rise to acute controversy, and is of greater significance in Africa than in the more advanced countries of Europe, is the right of union officers to be granted leave for trade union purposes. This is often provided for in collective agreements, which stipulate the conditions under which such leave is to be taken. Temporary absence of the union representative from normal work is generally based upon an agreement with the immediate manager as to its necessity and its regulation, but once established in principle, it becomes a matter of convention. Longer leave to enable trade-union officers to attend meetings, congresses of their organisations or even to travel overseas, is often regulated by specific agreement. Such leave is usually without pay, but employers who are keen to encourage responsible union activity are often generous in giving paid leave and such absences are never at the expense of the normal paid vacations. However, absence is usually, in form at any rate, subject to the needs of the company ; in English-speaking countries there is quite commonly a limit to the number of days allowed at any one time.[1]

The rights and obligations of the representatives of the workers in the undertaking are generally more extensively detailed in collective agreements than in legislation in the English-speaking countries. For example, the role and function of shop stewards are matters entirely for the unions and employers to establish by agreement and convention in the English-speaking territories. However, in the French-speaking territories *délégués du personnel* were, under the *Code du Travail* of 1952, a mandatory requirement in undertakings above a certain size. The method of their election, the size of their constituency, their terms of office, their functions and powers were all laid down in principle in Chapter III of the *Code* and given specific force by decree in each territory. Since independence this general pattern has been continued in the new codes.

In some of the most famous collective agreements in Britain the rights of the union and its representatives are balanced by a statement of the rights of the employer to manage his business without

---

[1] Under certain agreements in Ghana, for example, workers may be absent for three days on full pay to attend a national congress. Such an absence may last six days for two workers of the company appointed by the union under the collective agreement with the Shell Company in Nigeria.

interference in all respects other than those where negotiation rights have been conceded to the union. Similar statements of managerial prerogatives are to be found in agreements in the English-speaking countries of Africa.[1] Neither the labour codes nor collective agreements in the French-speaking countries mention the rights of the employer. This is because it is assumed that the employer has an implicit right to decide any issue unilaterally unless a union has been given a specific right to negotiate with the employer on the matter. Under the Anglo-Saxon tradition the rights of the employer and the union are the outcome of bargaining strength, mutual accommodation and convention rather than the application of law.

A similar sharp distinction occurs in the case of the preambles, which are quite a common feature of agreements in the English-speaking countries. These joint statements by the parties acknowledge their fundamental common interest in maintaining good industrial relations and affirm a joint readiness to improve the efficiency of the enterprise.[2] Such declarations of good intent are not to be found either in the labour codes or the collective agreements in the French-speaking countries. The reason for this absence is to be found in the French view of industrial relations which does not accept the notion that there exists a common interest between workers and employers. Neither unions nor management would find it easy to sign a declaration expressing mutual confidence in each other and a joint determination to achieve common goals. Mutual respect in the French tradition is a mutual respect for legal rights which is a matter of dedication to principle rather than accommodation of interests.

---

[1] 'The Union recognises that the Members of Association have the sole right to conduct their business and manage their operations, to control and direct the working forces, to introduce technical improvements, to determine the times, methods and manner of working and type of work to be done, and to modify, extend, curtail or cease operations and to determine the number of employees required ; to promote, demote, transfer and lay off employees and to discipline and discharge them for cause ; and to decide in their sole discretion all other matters connected with their business.' (Agreement between the Nigerian Plantation Employers' Association and the Nigerian Union of Plantation and Allied Workers, 1962.)

[2] For example, the following passage occurs in the 1960 transport agreement for the Adra, Tarzan and Khanji Companies in Ghana : 'The aim of this agreement is to establish satisfactory relations between (the workers and the management) . . . in the common desire to act in the interest of both parties with a view to promoting the economy of the company and the country generally and raising the standard of living and the welfare of the workers concerned'. In the 1963 agreement for plantation workers in Uganda the following terms are used : 'The parties to this agreement, having the common well-being of the timber trade at heart, agree to doing all in their power to promote stability of employment and productivity in the trade to the mutual benefit of both the employer and the employee'.

## LEGAL ASPECTS OF THE EMPLOYMENT RELATIONSHIP

Although in all the countries the conclusion, implementation, suspension and termination of individual contracts between workers and employers are in the main determined by legislation, these matters are also to a greater or lesser extent dealt with in collective agreements, which are often a good deal more favourable to the workers than the statutory provisions.

### Conclusion and Implementation of the Contract of Employment

The only limitations to the freedom of employers to hire whom they desire which are to be found in collective agreements are those that may have been brought about in certain cases by the intervention of the public authorities.[1]   Indeed many agreements explicitly recognise this principle and leave to the discretion of the employers such matters as the number of workers required for the various operations carried out by the enterprise and the scale of those operations.[2] However, a worker who is laid off when the size of the labour force is reduced, or who leaves his job to perform trade-union duties, often has to be given preference in employment in his own occupation for a period of six months to one year, or even two years subject to satisfactory completion of another trial period.[3]   In some cases the agreements state that to take advantage of such provisions the workers concerned must apply for re-engagement within a month of their termination of employment and must respond to any offer of a job by presenting themselves within the time limit specified by the employer ;[4] in other cases the latter undertakes not to hire other workers without first giving notice of his labour requirements to the trade union, which has a few days in which to assert the rights of the former personnel of the enterprise.[5]

Permanent employment is usually conditional on completion of a *probationary period*. Almost all the agreements fix a maximum duration for such a period, which may vary according to the occupational category of the worker and the place where he entered employment :

[1] The decision taken jointly in February 1964 by the employers' and workers' organisations and the Government of Kenya to increase by 10 per cent the staff of all the enterprises was a measure of exceptional urgency and should perhaps be viewed as the outcome of an official consultation with those organisations rather than of a negotiation in the usual sense of the term.       [2] See note 1, p. 88.
[3] Ivory Coast, agreement for the electricity and water supply industries.
[4] 1962 agreement of the COTONAF cotton company in the Central African Republic.                    [5] Uganda, civil engineering, 1964 agreement.

under the federal agreement for the construction industry in the former French West Africa the maximum is only one week for workers who are taken on locally and paid by the week, as against one month for salaried employees, three months for supervisors and six months for engineers, technicians and executive staff. In other cases, the accepted duration is uniformly three months, with a possible extension for another three. It seems that in countries where a maximum duration of the probationary period is laid down by law, the length is quite commonly reduced by agreement to the advantage of the workers, especially those in the lowest grades. The same clauses reserve the right of the parties to terminate probationary employment without notice or, in fewer but not exceptional cases, with a short period of notice (a week or two, or a month at the most).[1] These agreements confirm the employers' obligation to transform any probationary employment — if satisfactory — into regular employment at the end of the specified period, and provide that termination shall then be subject to the usual rules. Some of the agreements also state that a worker whose employment is confirmed at the end of the probationary period shall have his coverage by the agreement back-dated to the day when he was first employed.

Contrary to the practice for probationary periods, it is rare for *apprenticeship questions* to be dealt with by collective agreements, which do little more than refer to the regulations in force or to possible subsequent agreements. Sometimes, however, for instance in Sierra Leone and Ghana, they contain an undertaking by the management to promote the further general and technical education of the worker by the grant of fellowships or by other means. Some agreements in force in the latter country [2] include more detailed clauses on this point, which provide for : (1) the setting up in each undertaking of an apprenticeship committee consisting of two trade union officers and two experienced workers to study the problems of apprentice training and make recommendations ; (2) the opening and keeping by the employer of personal files with any relevant information on the training received ; and (3) the entrance of the worker, at the end of his term of apprenticeship, for tests organised by the Department of Labour and his assignment to work in the appropriate grade. It is also provided that the period of training shall be regarded as a period of employment for the purpose of calculating

---

[1] The following passage occurs, for example, in the petroleum industry agreement in Kenya : 'All employees on completion of the appropriate probationary period will be considered to have a contract period of one month'.
[2] The 1961 agreement for the printing trades.

length of service and granting the corresponding benefits.

Under agreements concluded in several countries, especially in West Africa, a worker whose employment has been confirmed is granted certain guarantees in respect of any *change in the terms of the personal contract of employment* which would reduce, during his period of service, the benefits granted to him under that contract. This may apply to the worker's grading or to other conditions of work. Changes are in this case subject to prior notice to be given to the worker in writing ; the worker is entitled to refuse the new terms proposed, and in that case the termination of his employment shall be deemed to be due to the employer. Temporary changes of job are not normally covered by such a rigid rule, but it may be specified that when a worker must perform for some time, at his employer's request, a job which has a lower grading than his normal one, his own previous grading and wage shall continue unchanged. Conversely, a worker who performs a more highly graded job on a provisional or temporary basis is often entitled, after a short time if not immediately, to receive additional remuneration and, after a certain specified period — as a rule four months in the French-speaking countries of Africa, three months in Ghana, six months in Nigeria — to be placed in the grade corresponding to that job or transferred back to his normal job.

In French-speaking Africa, too, the agreements make the transfer to another place of work (implying a change of residence) conditional on the worker's consent except where explicitly stated on hiring. In this respect some agreements concluded in other countries seem less liberal because they provide that a worker laid off because of a reduction of the labour force forfeits his right to a termination grant if he does not accept an equivalent job offered by the same firm in another establishment even though it may be located in a different town or municipality.[1]

*Promotion*, like initial employment, is left to the employer's decision even if the collective agreement provides, as it sometimes does, that promotion shall be granted on the basis of merit [2] or facilitated as much as possible by transfers to other parts of the undertaking.[3] However, the employer quite often undertakes to give preference in the event of a vacancy or the establishment of a job in a higher grade to workers already employed in the plant, provided they have the

---

[1] Uganda, motor trade industry, 1963 agreement.
[2] Agreement for the timber trade in Ghana.
[3] Agreement for the mines of Zambia (craftsmen).

necessary aptitudes.[1]  Under certain Ghana agreements [2] supervision
of the application of this undertaking is entrusted to a joint committee
of four which must interview candidates and communicate its findings
regarding the promotion to the management.  It is laid down in some
cases that possession of an official certificate of aptitude entitles the
holder to the corresponding grade if there is a vacancy in that grade.[3]

The implementation of an individual contract of employment
implies that the worker accepts the authority of the employer or his
representatives in all matters pertaining to *the organisation and
execution of work.*  This very general principle, which is explicitly
stated in some collective agreements, implies acceptance of discipline
involving penalties.  However, provisions concerning both organisation and penalties, which were previously to be found only in works
rules issued on their own authority by employers, have quite often
been included in agreements with the unions.

Work schedules are an example of this.  In principle they are
drawn up by the management to suit production needs.  However,
some agreements merely mention the times at which the working
day should normally begin and end, stipulating that the trade union
must receive advance notice of any proposed changes.  It may also
be laid down that for workers on shift work, hours must be fixed in
consultation with the representatives of the union.[4]  The workers are
sometimes allowed a certain amount of time off for shopping.[5]
Some agreements provide that overtime, which may normally be
imposed (within statutory limits) by the employer, requires the
worker's consent.[6]

As regards *discipline*, many agreements enumerate the penalties
applicable to the personnel (reprimand, suspension for one to eight
days and termination) ;  state the formalities to be complied with
(written notice, with a copy to the local labour inspector or to the
union) ;  reserve the possibility for the worker concerned to submit
written or oral explanations, often with the assistance of his representative ;  and fix a time limit (six months or one year) after which
measures such as a warning or suspension may no longer be invoked
for the application of a heavier penalty unless there has been a further
infringement of the rules.[7]

---

[1] Such an undertaking is found in most agreements of French-speaking Africa.
[2] Adra, Tarzan and Khanji companies (transport).
[3] Mining companies in Nigeria.    [4] Tanganyika Millers Co., 1963 agreement.
[5] Indian Merchant Association, Ghana, 1961 agreement.
[6] Terco Co., Ghana.
[7] These various points are covered in most of the former Federal agreements in
the French-speaking part of Africa, and are generally dealt with in the same terms

In addition to the acceptance of discipline within the enterprise, most agreements in French-speaking Africa include among the worker's obligations the giving up of all outside work that might in any way hinder the performance of his main function or compete with the business of the enterprise. As a rule the terms used are similar to those in the *Code du Travail* of 1952.[1] But whereas the *Code* provides that, when employment is terminated through the fault of the worker, the latter shall be subject to a non-competition clause for a period of two years and within a radius of 200 kilometres, many collective agreements give this clause narrower limits of time and space, restrict its application to the higher of grades of workers, or make it conditional on the payment of compensation.[2]

## Suspension of the Contract of Employment

The majority of collective agreements contain one or more clauses on interruptions of work linked with temporary circumstances beyond the worker's control and considered as grounds for suspension, but not termination, of the contract of employment.

Where such interruptions are due to *sickness*, *maternity* or *accident*, those clauses do little more than elaborate on the provisions of law in force in the country in question. They may, for instance, specify the justification that must be produced to the employer (medical certificate or examination by the works medical officer), or require the latter to examine, in conjunction with the representatives of the union, the possibility of regrading a worker whom sickness or accident has rendered unable to resume his former job. But they do not prolong the period during which a worker is entitled to resume his job where, as frequently happens, that period is fixed by law.[3] Their

in more recent agreements such as the agreement for the water and electricity supply industry of the Ivory Coast. Provisions that are similar in substance are found in a number of agreements in the English-speaking part of Africa, especially in Ghana, Kenya and Uganda.

[1] For example, the AOF Federal agreement for building and public works undertakings (already mentioned) reads as follows : 'Save as otherwise specified in the contract of employment or with the special permission of the employer no worker may engage, even outside working hours, in any trade or occupation that would compete with the business of the employer or hinder the effective discharge of the worker's obligations to the employer'.

[2] This type of limitation is found mostly in the commercial sector (Federal agreement for commerce in AOF ; agreement for the hotel trade in Ivory Coast, 1961).

[3] In the agreements of the French-speaking countries, as in the *Code* of 1952, the period is limited to six months or until another worker is given the job, whichever is the longer.

contribution consists essentially in conferring advantages of various kinds on the persons concerned during their absence from work. To these we shall revert later.

Another ground for suspension which is given more place in the collective agreements is *force majeure*. Very often the contracting parties define this in terms that cover a great variety of circumstances. The 1962 agreement for the Shell Company in the Sudan refers in this connection to emergencies and circumstances over which the worker has no control. The general labour agreement of Mauritania follows the example of a number of former federal agreements in recognising that if a short absence is justified by a serious and unforeseeable event, duly recorded, which directly affects the worker's home (e.g. if the worker's home catches fire or if his spouse or relatives in the ascending or descending line living with him are involved in a serious accident or fall seriously ill), the worker's employment shall not be terminated but simply suspended, provided that the employer has been notified within three days at the latest and that the duration of the worker's absence corresponds to the nature of the event which gave rise to it. The collective agreement for the COTONAF cotton firm in the Central African Republic refers in general terms to the keeping of a worker's job available — in suspension — in respect of absences that are duly notified, with valid reasons, that do not occur at unreasonable intervals and do not exceed three days, or even in respect of absences of more than three days in the event of recognised emergencies.

*Termination of Employment*

Termination of employment — whether due to the suppression of the job or to other causes — is a matter in respect of which collective agreements have made a particularly substantial contribution by extending and strengthening the statutory protection of the workers against arbitrary dismissals, and above all by mitigating the inevitable consequences of dismissals.

Although in principle the employer is everywhere free to decide in the matter of *collective dismissals*, as he is in the matter of initial employment, some collective agreements contain a restrictive enumeration of the reasons he may give in support of his decision. It seems, however, that only in Ghana are those reasons defined with any degree of precision. In several agreements concluded in that country the definition covers 'reorganisation of the undertaking,

94

exhaustion of the funds for a particular project, or completion of a project'. Elsewhere the notion of collective dismissal seems to be closely linked with that of a reduction in the scale of operations or an internal reorganisation of the undertaking, but the terms in which this is stated are too general to restrict the freedom of the employer to decide when the time is ripe for, or the scale of, collective dismissals.[1] In fact, the prerogatives conferred on the union representatives by the agreements are virtually limited, in this matter, to a right to receive advance notice.[2] They may further question, in accordance with the procedures laid down for examining individual complaints, whether there are good grounds for a decision to carry out a collective dismissal which they have reason to believe is dictated by other than economic considerations.[3]

Where a collective dismissal is unavoidable it is often laid down that the order of lay-offs shall be determined not only by the workers' personal qualities, but also in the light of their length of service in the establishment. However, the agreements never fail to state that the principle of 'last in, first out' is only applicable subject to equality of qualifications. In the English-speaking countries — Kenya and Nigeria, for instance — many agreements authorise the management to judge each worker's merits at its discretion. In the French-speaking countries instead, where the agreements lay down that a worker's family situation must also be taken into account and each dependent child adds a year to his seniority, the application of the principle in question is considered a matter for consultation between the employer and the staff delegates.

The law ordinarily provides that *notice* of dismissal shall be given, but it is the collective agreements that lay down the duration of the period of notice. In the French-speaking countries they take into

---

[1] For example, according to the 1963 agreement for the printing industry in Kenya, a redundancy exists 'when the undertaking has more employees than it can economically employ, a situation that may arise from mechanisation, rationalisation or a decrease in the activity of the undertaking due to economic or other causes'. In French-speaking Africa the agreements mention, without detail, a decrease in activity or reorganisation of the undertaking as recognised causes for collective dismissal.

[2] Thus, the Shell Company (Uganda) has undertaken to advise the union leaders a month in advance of any intention to reduce its payroll.

[3] 'The union agrees that the employers have the sole right to . . . suspend or terminate the services of any worker, whether he be a union member or otherwise, provided that this shall not preclude any worker involved from raising the matter of suspension or termination of service under the grievance procedure established in this agreement.' (Agreement between the Motor Trade and Allied Industries Association and the National Union of Clerical Commercial and Technical Employers of Uganda.) The matter might of course be raised even in the absence of a specific provision to that effect in the agreement.

account, as a rule, the worker's job category. For example, in the agreement for the electricity and water supply industry of the Ivory Coast, the period of notice for wage earners and salaried employees ranges from eight days to one month depending on the category ; it is one month for supervisors and three months for executive staff. In the English-speaking countries, where the agreements as a rule cover more uniform categories of workers, the period of notice, usually one month, may be the same for all the personnel of an enterprise, but it is generally shorter in those which employ a large proportion of unskilled manual workers. It may also vary with seniority : in Kenya, for instance, for the domestic staff in schools it ranges from one to two months after ten years' service and three months after twenty years. Sometimes workers belonging to the lower categories have the same notice as those in higher categories if they were recruited in remote districts.[1]

In accordance with a practice formerly recognised by the courts, but not normally provided for by law, very many agreements expressly reserve each party's right to compensation in lieu of notice corresponding to the remuneration and all other benefits which the worker would have received during the period of notice which is not actually respected. However, it is often laid down that a worker whose employment is terminated and who finds another job during the period of notice may leave his employment immediately without compensating the employer ;[2] likewise the employer may be explicitly released from any obligation towards a worker for whom he finds a new job with another employer at least as well paid as the old one.[3]

The labour codes in force in the French-speaking countries of Africa grant a worker, during the period of notice, one paid day off a week for the purpose of finding another job ; in these same countries collective agreements have quite commonly doubled this benefit by granting two hours a day with pay. The agreements state that a worker who agrees at the employer's request to forgo this right shall be paid a higher rate for the hours in question.

Besides any compensation that may be paid to a worker in lieu of notice, a high proportion of collective agreements provide that a worker whose employment is terminated by the employer shall

---

[1] AOF Federal agreement for building undertakings.
[2] This right is reserved in many agreements of the French-speaking countries and elsewhere (for example, in Sierra Leone for commercial employees). Sometimes the right is subject to the condition that at least half the period of notice has elapsed before a worker leaves. [3] Shell Company (Nigeria), 1961.

receive a *termination grant*. This grant, which has been viewed as a sort of deferred wage, is one of the major advantages that have accrued to the workers from the introduction of collective agreements. In fact, it is not as a rule provided for by law, even in the countries where the law has the most important part in establishing conditions of employment. To qualify, a worker must generally have been employed in the same undertaking for a specified period (one year or length of service at least equal to the qualifying period for entitlement to annual holidays). The amount depends on the worker's length of service in the undertaking. The Shell Company agreement in Nigeria provides that this grant shall amount to two weeks' wages for each year of continuous service beyond three, with an upper limit of one year's wages. It is more usual for the rate to increase with length of service : in the petroleum industry in Kenya — where the rates are particularly high — a worker is entitled to half a month's wages per year for the first five years of service, three-quarters of a month's wages for each succeeding year and one month's wages for each year of service beyond ten. Agreements in French-speaking countries in Africa almost all provide that in respect of each year spent in the undertaking the grant shall correspond to a specified percentage of the over-all average monthly remuneration received in the twelve months preceding the date of termination. The percentage in question is fixed at 20 per cent for the first five years, 25 per cent from the sixth to the tenth year and 30 per cent for every year after the tenth. To qualify for the grant under these agreements the worker's service must, as a rule, have been continuous, but lay-offs due to a reduction in the undertaking's payroll or to the intermittent character of the work (building industry) are not deemed to affect the continuity of employment for this purpose.

The agreements in force in the French-speaking countries provide that such a termination grant shall also be paid to workers whose employment is terminated as a result of a long illness and to any heirs of a deceased worker who were in fact dependent on the deceased. A worker's illness or death also imposes certain obligations on the employer (written notice of termination to a worker who falls ill or, where applicable, repatriation of a deceased worker's remains, at the family's request) which are sometimes laid down in the agreements concluded in those countries. In the other countries, instead, payment of a termination grant is mostly provided for only where the termination of the contract is due to the employer's decision to eliminate the job. However, in addition to the grant, some agreements provide that a worker whose employment is terminated for other reasons — without there being any fault on his part — shall receive a *long service gratuity*, the amount of which is calculated on a similar basis.[1]

Employment may be terminated without notice or compensation if the worker is guilty of serious misconduct. Most of the agreements examined reaffirm this principle, which has gained general acceptance. However, whereas some agreements (in the French-speaking parts of Africa) allow the competent court to determine the seriousness of the misconduct, others — many of them in Kenya and in Ghana — include detailed lists of the grounds that justify immediate dismissal.[2]

Under the regulations in force in a number of countries, every worker is entitled on request to receive a certificate when he leaves, whatever the reason for the termination of his employment. Some agreements have made the issue of such certificates to wage earners and salaried employees compulsory in all cases, and provide that the worker shall on request be issued with a provisional certificate at the beginning of the period of notice.

## WAGES AND RELATED BENEFITS

Remuneration has traditionally been the main subject of negotiation between employers' and workers' organisations. In Africa today, the need for a protection of the weakest categories of workers against the hardships of the labour market on the one side, and on the other the attempts made at developing an incomes policy, have

---

[1] A gratuity of this kind is stipulated, for instance, in the Singer Company agreement in Kenya. It is somewhat lower than the termination grant, except for workers who have been employed in the enterprise for a very long time.

[2] For example, the following are recognised in collective agreements in Ghana (e.g. for the timber trade) as making a worker liable to dismissal without notice :
 (1) flagrant disregard of the contents of the agreement ;
 (2) imparting information prejudicial to the employer's interests ;
 (3) accepting bribes to the detriment of the employer's interests or in order to misuse authority ;
 (4) conduct endangering the lives or safety of other persons, causing loss of, or damage to, the employer's property, or seriously affecting the progress of work ;
 (5) stealing and pilfering or attempted fraud ;
 (6) sleeping on duty ;
 (7) dereliction of duty ;
 (8) consuming alcohol or drink on duty ;
 (9) smoking in a prohibited area ;
 (10) refusal to comply with a reasonable order.

imposed more or less strong limitations upon the free settlement of wages. Statutory minimum rates, the paramount importance of which in French-speaking countries has been stressed, and which also govern rather large territorial or occupational areas in English-speaking countries, are in fact applied without significant modifications to a high proportion of the unskilled, even in sectors covered by agreements. At the same time pressures from the privileged groups — and it has been advanced, probably with some exaggeration, that all persons working for wages belonged to such groups — have not been allowed to be exerted without restraint. In spite of these limitations, remuneration is still a major topic in negotiations ; and even in those cases where increases in the level of cash earnings has been restrained, the agreements have made a significant contribution to the determination of the wage structure and the increase of related benefits.[1]

Except for the preliminary agreements on recognition and procedure and those sometimes concluded separately, in the English-speaking countries, to govern certain special points in the relations between the employer and the workers in his employ, all collective agreements devote more or less attention to remuneration. The scale of wage rates for the various job categories is usually included in the text of the agreement or in a schedule to it. However, this is not the case in the French-speaking countries, where, as we have seen, wages and general conditions of employment are often fixed at different levels. The national industry-wide collective agreements, after recalling that 'the minimum wage rates for each category are determined and revised by a joint committee consisting of equal numbers of employers and workers belonging to the organisations which have signed the agreement',[2] merely state the general principles governing remuneration and leave the actual rates to be fixed by additional agreements covering a more limited geographical area.

The first of these principles is that there must be an equitable *relationship between the wage and the type of job* the worker does in the enterprise. This has resulted in most collective agreements including a job classification, in which each grade corresponds to a certain hourly or a weekly wage rate that may or may not be mentioned in the document in question.

---

[1] In the next pages we shall be concerned mainly with the structure of wages and fringe benefits ; an economic description of wage levels would go beyond the limits of the present study.

[2] The wording is reproduced from former federal agreements in several recent agreements, including the general agreement of 1962 for Mauritania.

In French-speaking countries, the job classifications which are included in the agreements, or schedules to them, are particularly detailed. They generally comprise, for workers in each of the trades in the industry in question (e.g. in building and public works, carpentry, electricity, tile laying, etc.), from six to eight categories, ranging from 'ordinary labourer', that is to say 'a worker who is given simple tasks requiring no trade knowledge or adjustment', to 'skilled worker performing tasks that call for extensive theoretical and practical training', while 'exceptionally able workers doing work of a high standard in a particular craft, especially work of an artistic character', are in a category apart. Salaried employees and supervisory, executive and technical staff are also divided into a certain number of classes. At every level the tasks corresponding to the particular category are listed and briefly but accurately described,[1] so that even when they provide no direct information on rates of remuneration, the agreements in question do at least have the advantage of giving an over-all view of the occupational structure.

A very detailed description of jobs can also be found in some agreements in the English-speaking countries.[2] But as a rule the workers they cover — even when the jobs they do are very different — are divided into fewer, more comprehensive groups and the mere mention of their craft is considered sufficient to determine their level on the wage scale.[3] A method often followed in enterprises where the difference in the level of qualifications and remuneration is relatively small, consists in grouping the various jobs under three heads — 'unskilled', 'semi-skilled' and 'skilled'.[4] Elsewhere we find that the agreement does not contain a scale of wages but merely quotes a rate of increase over the wage previously paid [5] or over the statutory minimum wage for the various areas covered by the operations of a group of enterprises.[6] This increase is sometimes a percentage instead of an absolute figure, in which case the agreement

[1] An interesting example of such descriptions will be found in the recent agreements for the hotel trade in Senegal (1960) and the Ivory Coast (1961).
[2] The most remarkable of these examples is undoubtedly that offered by the long-standing agreement for the specialised workers in the Zambia mines mentioned in the previous chapter. There are some others, particularly in the agreements for the motor vehicle sales and service firms in Uganda, the timber industry in Ghana and the mines in Nigeria.
[3] Thus in the agreement for the Singer Company (1963) in Kenya, the whole staff — from office boys through drivers and mechanics to secretaries — is divided into eight categories each of which corresponds to a certain type of job.
[4] Example : the Bulleys tanneries in Kenya ; in this enterprise the differential between the first and third categories is not more than 30 per cent.
[5] Agreement for the unskilled miners in Zambia.
[6] Agreement for building and civil engineering in Uganda (1964).

may lay down that the entire wage structure shall be revised so as to show the same percentage increase at all levels.[1]

Another principle embodied in every system of remuneration in keeping with modern ideas is summed up in the words '*equal pay for equal work*'. In many collective agreements in the French-speaking countries it is couched in the particularly explicit wording of the *Code* of 1952 : 'provided their work, qualifications and output are the same, all workers shall receive the same wage, irrespective of their origin, sex, age and status'. The same agreements provide, however, that the remuneration of non-adult workers shall be subject to a reduction ranging from 10 per cent between 17 and 18 years of age to 40 per cent between 14 and 15 years of age. The agreements state that this reduction shall not apply to young workers who hold a trade certificate, or, more generally, to those who normally do work usually entrusted to adults, and whose speed, output and quality of work are the same. A reduction in wages is sometimes also allowed for physically handicapped workers, but in such cases the reduction may not exceed 10 per cent of the normal wage for the worker's grade.

The agreements in force in the other countries seldom deal with this aspect of the remuneration problem. Some of them exempt the employer from applying the stipulated minimum rate to workers less than 18 years of age. However, they guarantee those workers the same wage as the others when they do the same job, though laying down that minors shall not, in principle, be allocated full adult tasks. On other points, the principle of non-discrimination has sometimes been more seriously jeopardised. Thus, under the terms of the agreement concluded in Kenya in 1961 between the Agricultural Workers' Union and the National Farmers' Union, women, as a general rule, can demand only half the wage of male workers. It is hard to say whether this inequality is warranted by a difference of the same magnitude in the weight of the tasks women are allocated or actually perform. In other undertakings the margin between the pay rates for the two sexes, though not so great, is still considerable.[2] In most cases, however, the collective agreement quotes a single rate for each job category and if women actually receive a lower wage the reason probably lies in the fact that they are allocated less well paid work or are less able to meet the current productivity standards.

[1] Agreement for the mines in Liberia (1964).
[2] In Kenya, for example, this margin is of 25 per cent in tanneries and 20 per cent in the food-processing industries.

It is also through a difference in productivity and, more particularly, in qualification that in most countries African workers remain in a less favourable situation than others, long after all forms of discrimination based on birth or occupational status have disappeared from the laws and from rules of the workers' organisations. Indeed, current developments in this respect seem to be linked not with a change in the agreed systems of remuneration, but with the progressive Africanisation of the specialised labour force and the executive and technical staff — a process which the parties to some collective agreements explicitly undertake to make every effort to promote.

Many collective agreements provide for a *wage increase corresponding to length of service*. In conjunction with other benefits already mentioned, such as a higher termination grant, it completes the range of means included in the agreements for encouraging workers to remain with an undertaking. Unlike upgrading, which depends, as we have seen, on a vacancy in a higher grade job and on the employer's discretion, the annual increment for each grade is considered, as a rule, to be more or less automatic. Sometimes, for instance in Ghana and Liberia, the employer reserves the right to suspend the annual increment for a worker whose conduct is not satisfactory ; in the first of these two countries, several agreements compel the employer to give the worker and the union advance notice in writing of any decision he intends to take to cancel the annual increment. It is sometimes laid down that the annual increments of particularly deserving workers shall be larger than normal. In the French-speaking countries, the seniority bonus is calculated, as a rule, as a percentage of the basic wage for each grade ; it never amounts to more than 1 per cent of that figure per year (limited to 12 or 15 years) ; there are detailed provisions on the calculation of the length of service, with a list of cases in which absence is not to be regarded as an interruption of the period of service (not more than six months' illness, employment injury however long-lasting, period of vocational training) and of cases in which several successive periods spent in the undertaking may be lumped together for the purpose of qualifying for the bonus and calculating the amount due (case of departures caused by reductions in the undertaking's labour force). In the other countries the progression, which is mostly due to the application of a schedule of increasing rates, is usually steeper at the start — quite often it comes very close to 5 per cent a year — but is kept within limits of the same order (15 to 20 per cent). Very exceptionally it leads to a far greater increase over the initial wage for workers of a given grade.[1]

End-of-year bonuses are in some respects similar to seniority bonuses ; some agreements provide for them, and the amount also sometimes depends on length of service.[2] However, there are many cases in which the bonus is the same for all workers with at least one year of service.

Several agreements expressly recognise in general terms the employer's right to introduce any system of payment (piece work, task work or other forms of payment by results) which he may consider to be in the interest of the undertaking, provided that 'the worker shall always be assured of receiving a wage at least equal to the minimum for his occupational category' and that 'measures shall be taken to prevent any over-work by personnel paid by results', but the methods of calculating and applying *productivity standards* are not otherwise specified. Schemes for interesting the staff collectively in the results of the enterprise or a production unit are still very rare. An example is offered by the 1962 Shell Company agreement in Sudan, under which the workers in a container factory receive additional remuneration, corresponding to a specified number of hours of overtime, when the number of containers produced reaches a certain level.

The role of collective agreements with regard to *overtime pay* seems to be more important and more constant. In some undertakings overtime is paid at the same rate as normal time when it does not exceed a specified number of hours.[3] But it is far more usual for all overtime work to be paid at a higher rate. The increase is sometimes fixed at 25 per cent of the standard rate, but as a rule in the English-speaking countries it is 50 per cent on weekdays and 100 per cent on Sundays and holidays, as well as sometimes on weekdays after a certain number of hours. In the French-speaking countries the agreements have introduced a progressive system (increase of 10 per cent for the first eight hours beyond 40 and 35 per cent thereafter ; 50 per cent for night work and work on Sundays and public holidays and 100 per cent for night work on Sundays and public holidays). This system is generally more favourable to the worker than the statutory provisions in force.

On the other hand, many agreements stipulate *extra pay for jobs involving special conditions, difficulties or dangers.*

[1] In the Shell Company (Sierra Leone) agreement, the increase reaches 50 per cent after periods from 9 to 18 years according to the workers' category.
[2] Several agreements in Ghana, and the agreement for agriculture in Somalia.
[3] The limit is one hour in certain undertakings in Kenya.

For instance, as compensation for the drawbacks of shift work those involved may receive a special hourly bonus added to the basic wage.[1] This bonus is sometimes higher for workers whose shifts change over at frequent intervals.[2] In the French-speaking countries of Africa workers who do at least six hours of night work receive an allowance equal to twice the hourly wage of an ordinary labourer.

Particularly hazardous or unhealthy work is frequently paid for at a higher rate. Many agreements in the English-speaking countries of Africa grant special allowances for jobs done under exceptionally bad conditions, e.g. near boilers, or in exceptionally dangerous places. Thus, men working above a certain height are usually granted a 'height allowance'.[3] In the French-speaking countries there is a tendency to provide in more general terms, at the level of the branch of industry — e.g. the timber trade in the Ivory Coast — for the granting of bonuses additional to the wage 'to take account of special working conditions when such conditions have not been taken into consideration in determining the wages of the workers concerned, especially for dangerous work or unhealthy work involving risk of illness or special strain on the constitution'. The amount of these bonuses has to be determined by supplementary agreements. Special allowances may also be payable, on occasion, for exceptionally dirty work involving an unusual degree of wear and tear on clothing (when working clothes are not supplied by the employer). The same applies to work done with the worker's own tools.[4]

Workers who have to work temporarily at a place other than the usual place of work normally receive a *displacement* allowance of an amount fixed in most of the agreements according to the basic wage for the particular category ; instead of such a lump-sum grant the exact additional expense incurred may be refunded for more senior personnel. Certain agreements, especially in the French-speaking parts of Africa, provide that when the displacement is to last for more than a certain time (six months) the worker may be accompanied or

[1] Agreement for the petroleum industry in Kenya.
[2] Agreement for the mines of Zambia (craftsmen).
[3] In Ghana, in the timber trade, this bonus amounts to 25 per cent of the normal wage when the work is done at a height of more than 100 feet, whereas in the building industry the rate varies according to a detailed scale, in accordance with the height.
[4] The tool allowance is for example one penny an hour under the agreement for the mines of Zambia (craftsmen), which also provides that every apprentice shall be credited with a similar sum on the company's books for the purchase of any tools he may wish. Under the building agreement in Ghana (September 1961) the amount of the allowance varies according to the trade. A list of the tools the worker must have to be entitled to the allowance is appended to this agreement.

# The Content of Collective Agreements

joined by his family, travelling at the employer's expense, and he is
also to receive the remuneration which he used to receive at his usual
place of employment, if such remuneration was higher than the
amount paid at the place of temporary transfer. When it takes
place at the employer's request, definitive *transfer* from one place of
work to another gives rise, in other countries as well, not only to the
reimbursement of travelling expenses but also to the payment of a
special allowance which is generally of a smaller amount ; this allowance may consist in a single payment, of a rather moderate sum,[1]
or in a daily bonus for one month following the transfer.[2] Finally,
account is often taken, in fixing wage rates, of a factor which is often
of particular importance in Africa, namely the distance between the
worker's home (where he is recruited) and his place of employment.
In the French-speaking part of Africa, the circumstances in which a
distance or expatriation allowance shall be payable have been defined
in detail by regulations made under section 94 of the *Code du Travail*
of 1952, but in many cases these definitions have been relaxed by
collective agreements which extend payment of the allowance to
any worker usually resident at a distance of 500 kilometres or more,
and specify a certain amount.[3] Under these agreements the employer
is also compelled to pay the statutory deposit for the worker's
repatriation, and the circumstances in which a worker may claim
reimbursement of his travelling expenses for the return journey are
specified. The agreements also determine, according to the worker's
grade, the class of travel to which he is entitled for himself and his
family and the weight of the luggage that may be carried at the
employer's expense.

Under some collective agreements the employers undertake, in
addition to the cash wage, to supply their workers with certain
*benefits in kind*, such as housing, food, clothing or uniforms, transport
facilities, or goods or services connected with the business of the
undertaking.[4] In some undertakings, particularly in the agricultural
sector, *housing* has traditionally been made available to the workers.

---

[1] 15 per cent of the basic monthly wage in the timber industry in Ghana ; a
lump sum of £12–15 for the oil companies' salaried employees in Nigeria and
Sierra Leone.
[2] Shell Company agreement (Uganda).
[3] For example, under the general agreement for Mauritania the allowance
amounts to 5 per cent of the workers' basic wage for every 500 kilometres as the
crow flies between his usual place of residence and the place of employment
(subject to a ceiling of 20 per cent of the basic wage).
[4] For example, under the agreement for the electricity and water production and
distribution industry of the Ivory Coast, a specified amount of electric current for
household use.

In others, including quite a large number in Kenya, it is replaced by a special allowance.[1]  In Liberia the agreement for the mining industry signed in 1964 provides for the setting up of a building programme which should in the following four years supply housing for all miners not already housed.  In the French-speaking countries laws and regulations provide that adequate housing shall be made available to workers who have to move for occupational reasons, and on this subject the agreements merely go into more detail, particularly with regard to the time a worker is to be given to vacate the premises if his employment is terminated (the time varies according to the grounds for termination, as in the case of notice).  The agreements also specify that the housing must meet the needs of the worker and his family, due regard being paid to the customs and facilities at the place of employment.  *Food* supplied under the collective agreements in certain industries (in particular the hotel industry) is part of the worker's regular remuneration rather than a supplementary benefit, and a cash payment must be made if the food is not supplied.[2]  In other cases, for instance the agricultural undertakings in Kenya, it is stipulated that rations shall be deducted from the cash wage in an amount calculated in accordance with clearly defined principles.[3]  The grant of *clothing* makes up for the worker's obligation to replace garments that wear out quickly, or to wear a uniform.  Clothing is issued in accordance with rules corresponding to the nature of the work.[4]

## SOCIAL BENEFITS

Some countries have no government social assistance or security schemes, while in many others such schemes are still at a rudimentary stage.  This has quite naturally led the trade union organisations to take initiatives with a view to extending the duties of the employers in the social field.

[1] The workers in the Bulleys tanneries in Kenya receive a housing allowance of 24 shillings (1963 agreement).  In the engineering industry the allowance ranges between 15 and 20 shillings a month, depending on the worker's grading.

[2] The 1960 agreement for the hotel industry in Senegal states that the food provided for the workers is to be 'wholesome, plentiful and varied'.

[3] The general agreement concluded in 1961 for the undertakings affiliated to the National Farmers' Union in Kenya provides that products purchased outside the undertaking by the employer shall be made available at retail prices and those produced in the undertaking at the prices paid by wholesalers.

[4] Under the 1963 agreement for the tobacco industry in the Sudan, for example, three uniforms are to be supplied to all workers every year, and this number is raised to four for workers on particularly dirty work.

## The Content of Collective Agreements

The provisions most generally adopted in this sphere provide for *compensation, totally or in part, to sick workers for the loss of their normal wage.*

The sum which the employer is required to pay to sick workers in the French-speaking countries under the *Code du Travail* (allowance equal to the amount of the worker's remuneration for a period corresponding to the period of notice) is increased by agreements in these countries to an unequal, but always considerable, extent which varies according to the worker's length of service. To the statutory minimum the 1959 agreement for the building and public works industries in the Republic of the Congo (Brazzaville) adds half pay for 2 months for workers whose length of service amounts to between 5 and 10 years, for 3 months after 10 years, for 4 months after 15 years and for 5 months after 20 years, provided that the total allowance does not amount to more than 6 months' wages. In Mauritania the general agreement of 1963, like the most liberal agreements formerly concluded in French West Africa, goes further : besides full pay for a period equal to the period of notice, this agreement provides for half pay for 3 months as from the very first year spent in the undertaking ; senior workers receive full pay for a period equal to twice the period of notice and half pay for 4 months, plus a quarter of a month's wages for every 2 years of employment in the undertaking after the 5th.

In the English-speaking part of Africa the differences between one country and another and between one undertaking and another in the same country are much greater than are found in the French-speaking countries. Under most of the agreements, in the event of sickness a worker receives his full wage for a certain maximum number of days a year, and half his wage for an additional period equal to, or quite often longer than, the former. In one undertaking in Kenya these periods never exceed 7 days each, while in another they amount to no less than 60 days. However, in that country as in the others of the same group, intermediate terms (from 15 to 30 days) occur more frequently. As a rule, a minimum period of service, which in many cases is identical with the probation period, is stipulated. But in general, length of service is of no account ; [1] this is just the contrary of the usage in the French-speaking countries. Sometimes the worker's grading is taken into consideration : in Ghana, for example,

[1] This rule is by no means universal. An exception is the agreement for the Shell Company in Sierra Leone, under which periods of sick leave with full and half pay, amounting to 1 month each for workers with less than 5 years' service, are increased to 2 months after 5 years with the undertaking and to 2½ months after 10 years.

salaried employees in the timber trade are entitled in the event of sickness, after 12 months of continuous service, to their full pay for 30 days and half pay for a further 30 days ; for workers in lower grades the two periods are reduced to a fortnight.

Lastly, whereas it is always accepted — and sometimes explicitly laid down — that after a certain length of time (usually 6 months) sickness entitles the employer to terminate the contract of employment, many agreements provide that 'cases of long illness shall be given special consideration by the management'.

Collective agreements seem so far to have been less important in the sphere of *maternity* and *industrial accidents*. It is true that some of those concluded in the English-speaking countries group maternity with sickness as far as benefits are concerned,[1] or grant a more or less considerable fraction of the normal wage during the twelve weeks of authorised absence from work.[2] But still more numerous, in those countries, are the agreements which, while mentioning that the person in question is entitled to leave of absence and recalling, on occasion, that she must be reinstated at the end of such leave without forfeiting any of the rights acquired during past service, provide that she shall not receive any wage until she returns to work. Where the agreements mention accidents, as a rule they merely refer back to the provisions of the national legislation.

In the French-speaking countries the benefits laid down by law for women workers who bear children (payment of half wage during fourteen weeks' leave) do not appear to have been augmented by the agreements. Instead, many of the latter grant an injured worker, for the period during which compensation is payable to a sick worker, an allowance sufficient to cover his former wage less the sum due him for the same period under the regulations on industrial accidents.

In addition to allowances paid to make up for the loss of the normal wages, collective agreements sometimes place employers under an obligation to meet the *expenses arising out of sickness, accidents or maternity*. In the French-speaking countries agreements generally grant a worker who goes to hospital entitlement to a daily allowance which varies according to the basic wage (three times the hourly rate). They also provide that the employer shall pay a deposit (subject to certain limitations) for hospital expenses. In other coun-

---

[1] Agreements for the Singer Company in Kenya and road transport in Ghana.
[2] This fraction is one-half in the Shell Company in Sierra Leone, one-third in commercial undertakings in that country, and one-quarter in certain oil companies in Kenya. In some cases maternity leave is limited to 6 weeks.

tries — particularly Nigeria, Ghana, Tanzania and Kenya [1] — certain
agreements lay down that the employer shall meet the cost not only
of care in case of accident covered by national legislation, but also
of medical examinations and treatments provided in other cases by
Government or company hospitals — although reimbursement may
be limited to a fixed percentage of the expenditure,[2] or certain classes
or expenditure (maternity expenses, dental care, purchase of spec-
tacles, as well as expenses arising out of misconduct or negligence on
the part of the wage earner) may be excluded. Outside the French-
speaking part of Africa, however, it seems more usual to limit the
payments to be made by the undertaking to a sick worker to the
payment of the wage, subject to the above-mentioned conditions and
restrictions.

As regards medical care and the prevention of sickness and accidents, it will be noted that certain aspects of the health and medical
organisation of the undertaking are sometimes covered by collective
agreements. For example, the federal agreement for the building
and public works industry of French West Africa provides that
certain categories of undertakings are to have the staff and the health
facilities which are statutorily provided for in respect of larger
undertakings. The above-mentioned agreement for the Ivory Coast
establishes a joint health and safety committee under the chairmanship of the manager of the undertaking, which is empowered to
carry out any inquiries or checks and to make any suggestions which
may be required in this field. However, occupational safety and
hygiene are normally ensured primarily by appropriate Government
regulations, and few agreements include detailed provisions on this
subject.[3]

Worthy of mention among the social measures already introduced
or prepared for by collective bargaining, though they are rather the
exception than the rule, is the setting up of *provident or pension funds*
to which the employers undertake to make certain contributions.[4]
As a matter of fact, the agreements concluded so far which contain
provisions on this point, do not lay down detailed conditions concerning present or future schemes, but rather reflect an accord in

[1] See in particular the agreements for mines in Nigeria, for several road transport companies in Ghana, for commercial firms (Balfour Beatty Co.) in Kenya.
[2] For example, the percentage is 75 per cent at the Total Oil Company (Nigeria).
[3] As an example of such provisions mention may be made of those in the agreement for the mines of Zambia which relate to the protective equipment to be provided for their workers (craftsmen) by companies that are parties to the agreement.
[4] For instance, under the agreement of 1962 the mining companies in Nigeria
have doubled their wage earners' contributions to a sick fund.

principle preparing the way to further discussions. In a few cases, however, a proper pension scheme has been established by collective bargaining.[1] On the other hand, as mentioned earlier, the pension to which a worker may be entitled under national legislation is supplemented, under several agreements concluded in the French-speaking part of Africa, by the payment of a retirement grant of an amount corresponding to a specified percentage of the termination grant.

## HOURS OF WORK AND HOLIDAYS

*Daily and weekly hours of work* are in a number of countries determined, sometimes in great detail, by national legislation. In the French-speaking countries collective agreements add little to the law, to which they usually do no more than refer, or the terms of which they reproduce, with regard not only to normal hours of work but also to such matters as making up for time lost through collective stoppages of work, or special conditions for workers who are required to remain available at their homes at specified times outside working hours. In the other countries, however, weekly hours are usually stated in the agreements. It should be noted that these hours may vary considerably within a particular country — from $39\frac{1}{2}$ (Shell Company) to 48 (civil engineering, plantations) in Uganda, for example. Without claiming to lay down a general rule, it may be said that in industry the working week amounts usually to between 42 and 45 hours, that it is often slightly shorter for salaried workers,[2] and that it mostly reaches 48 hours in agriculture.[3]

Collective agreements in practically all countries have made an important contribution in the field of *annual holidays*. The minimum duration of such holidays is almost always laid down by law, but there are very many agreements which provide for longer holidays corresponding to length of service : annual holidays may be increased, for instance, from 12 to 26 days after 25 years' service [4] or, more usually,

[1] See schedule to the federal collective agreement for building undertakings and to several other federal agreements (the schedule was published in the *Journal officiel de l'Afrique occidentale française*, 29 April 1958), and the 1961 agreements for the mining industry (mineworkers and staff employees) in (Southern) Rhodesia.

[2] In Nigeria, for instance, instead of the 44 and 46 hours respectively for wage earners in the Total and Shell companies, salaried workers do only 40 hours a week in the former and 42 hours in the latter.

[3] It would seem, however, that in practice the daily stint allotted to plantation workers in many cases allows them to leave work before the normal time.

[4] Shops and offices in Sierra Leone.

from 2 to 3 weeks after 5 or 10 years. In other cases longer holidays are a matter of grade rather than years of service : this applies in particular to the banks in Madagascar (2 to 4 days of extra holidays for executive and technical staff), to the Bank of West Africa in Ghana (holidays ranging from 15 to 28 days according to the grade), and to the mines in Nigeria (from 16 to 40 days every 2 years). Seniority and grading are sometimes both taken into consideration.[1] In several countries of West Africa the normal holiday for workers from distant parts is raised from 1½ days (statutory minimum) to 2 working days per month of actual work. If a temporary transfer is extended beyond 6 months, a worker whose family has remained at his usual place of employment may receive a paid holiday to go back to his family for 2 or 3 days every 2 or 3 months. The agreements also often contain practical provisions for fixing holiday dates (by consultations between the parties). They sometimes provide for a special holiday or travel allowance.[2]

*Public holidays* are often listed in collective agreements. In accordance with statutory provisions such a list may be adjusted to allow in particular for religious factors. Sometimes there is a choice between Christian and Moslem holidays.

A common characteristic of the great majority of the agreements under examination consists in very liberal provisions (as compared with those of agreements for non-African countries) with regard to *special leave*. Reference has already been made to the fairly wide definition of *force majeure* as legitimate justification for absence from work.[3] The right to special leave is fairly commonly reserved for workers in respect of events in their personal or family lives. The duration of such leave is commonly fixed in French-speaking countries at 2 days for a worker's marriage, 1 or 2 days for the marriage or funeral of a member of his family and 1 day for the birth of a child and for its christening. Such leave may not total more than 10 days a year ; remuneration is not affected. In English-speaking countries special leave may be granted in circumstances which are less strictly

---

[1] Under the agreement for the timber trade in Ghana, 2 weeks' holidays a year are due after 1 year of service for workers earning less than £240 and 3 weeks are due to the others, while workers earning more than £420 qualify for 4 weeks after 10 years of service. In the Sudan (agreement for the tobacco industry, 1963), annual holidays comprise 15 days for workers in the first category, 15 to 21 according to seniority in the second category and 21 to 30 in the third and fourth categories.
[2] In the agreements which grant such an allocation, this varies from £3 to £10 according to grade and family status.
[3] See above, the section dealing with the suspension of a worker's employment.

I

defined, such as to deal with urgent personal business or for the celebration of appropriate religious holidays, but as a rule workers are not paid for such leave, or it is deducted from the annual holiday.[1]

[1] Exceptions to this rule are found in several agreements in Ghana and the Sudan. The 1962 agreement for Nigerian mines leaves it to the employer to decide in each case whether special leave should be paid or not.

Chapter 6

# THE IMPLEMENTATION OF COLLECTIVE AGREEMENTS

THE implementation of collective agreements raises a number of legal and practical problems in the solution of which law, usage and accord play their part. But that part is not the same on each side of the borderline which divides, within the modern sector of the African economies, the countries that follow different traditions. As a rule it has been found necessary to include specific clauses covering the implementation of collective agreements ; but whereas such clauses play a predominant or exclusive part in the English-speaking countries, in the others they do little more than round out the imperative principles laid down by law. For all this diversity of approach, however, the solutions adopted on both sides of the line have quite a number of points in common because they are designed to meet very similar conditions. In this chapter an attempt is made to present a general survey of these solutions, taking into account all the various factors that help to determine them.

The first problem is to define the scope of application of a collective agreement. Who exactly are the people bound by it ? A first reply to this question was given above when the bargaining procedures were examined, since the level selected for negotiating an agreement determines the size of the groups whose relations it is designed to govern. But the situation in a given sector or undertaking of the workers or employers who did not take part in the negotiations, either personally or by delegation, has still to be clarified.

The time factor in the application of a collective agreement also calls for some comment with regard not only to its period of validity but also to such matters as the procedures for its termination (if any are fixed), its impact on previously concluded contracts of employment, etc.

Lastly, the application of collective agreements also involves the problem of their moral and legal authority and sanction. After an attempt to clarify the theoretical aspects of this problem, mention will be made of some of the difficulties most commonly encountered in the daily implementation of collective agreements and a brief description of the machinery set up in the different countries for overcoming them will be given.

## THE GROUP OF PEOPLE CONCERNED : CONTRACTING AND NON-CONTRACTING PARTIES

The definition of the group of people covered by a collective agreement — and more precisely how far that agreement must be considered applicable to non-members of trade unions or associations — is a matter of prime importance.  Firstly, because very often only a minute percentage of workers can be viewed as regular union members, even where the majority acknowledge with more or less certainty a particular union as their normal representative ; secondly, because the employers' organisations are still far from covering all undertakings despite the rapid progress they have made in recent years.

Under the terms of the *Code du Travail* of 1952, or of those that have replaced it in many French-speaking countries, a collective agreement — even if it cannot be or has not been extended — is applicable to all the workers on the payroll of an employer who is bound by it.  Owing to the existence and gradual generalisation of industry-wide agreements, the application of this principle would very often suffice, without the need for special Government action, to give a collective agreement virtually the same coverage as an order.

Generally speaking, no rule of this sort is laid down in the laws of the English-speaking countries.  Ghana, where it has been incorporated in the Labour Relations Act 1958, is an exception.  But even in these countries a collective agreement is viewed, in accordance with well-established usage, as applicable to all the workers in the undertakings concerned — or at least to all those who belong to the categories whose spokesman the signatory union is held to be — whether they are regular members or not.  This does not seem to raise any particular difficulties, even where the percentage of contribution payers is low (and thanks to the check-off system it is often higher than elsewhere).  After all, to grant less favourable conditions to non-union members would seem to be incompatible with the provisions of the law or the clauses of the agreements, such as frequently occur in all countries, laying down that an employer in his relations with his staff must not take into consideration whether or not they belong to a union.

A more serious limitation to the effect of a collective agreement may derive from the fact that an employer who is neither a party to it nor a member of a signatory organisation cannot be held *a priori* to be bound by it. Indeed, though it is hard to imagine the possibility of discrimination — even where not explicitly banned by a clause in the law or agreement — between members and non-members of a union in the same undertaking, there may be many cases where an employer remains voluntarily aloof from the employers' organisation in his region or sector of industry for the precise purpose of not fulfilling the obligations it has undertaken. That this is a very real possibility is demonstrated by the position taken until quite recently by many heads of small agricultural or industrial concerns even in a country as advanced in the practice of labour relations as Kenya.

That is the reason for the measures taken in several countries to facilitate, or if necessary enforce, the application of collective agreements by a larger group of employers than that constituted by the signatories alone.

The legal codes in force in French-speaking Africa provide, in general terms, that any association or employer not a party to a collective agreement may adhere to it subsequently. In some of the agreements concluded in those countries the formal requirements for and effects of adherence are governed by a special clause which, as a rule, lays down the rights of the adhering organisations or individuals (as regards the possibility of denouncing or revising the agreement and participating in joint bodies set up under it) in somewhat more restrictive terms than those of the original signatories. On the other hand, even without their formal adherence, all employers who at any time become members of a signatory organisation accept the obligations it has undertaken towards the workers (whereas no employer can evade these obligations by leaving the organisation of which he was a member at the time the agreement was concluded).

In addition to such measures whose application implies the explicit consent of the parties concerned, the laws of several countries contain others that restrict the freedom of action of non-signatory employers. The laws most commonly met with empower the administration to 'extend' a collective agreement ; namely to declare all or some of its clauses applicable to all the employers and workers in a certain sector of industry or a certain territorial area. This power has long been recognised in all the countries of French-speaking Africa subject to the conditions mentioned above [1] (negotiation of the agreement in an

[1] See chapter on negotiating procedures.

*ad hoc* committee by the most representative employers' and workers' organisations ; consultation of all concerned prior to the Minister's decision). More recently this power has been conferred on the authorities concerned with labour problems in several other countries. The system adopted in Ghana closely resembles that provided for in the labour codes of the neighbouring countries, in that the extension orders postulate that the organisations which signed the agreement in question were sufficiently representative of the employers and workers concerned and that appropriate publicity at an early stage gave all those interested the opportunity to express their views. However, in the Industrial Relations Act 1958, the initiative for an extension measure rests with the Minister alone. In (Southern) Rhodesia the agreements negotiated in the industrial councils — like those which in Sierra Leone stem from decisions of the joint industrial councils — are likewise capable of extension, at the Minister's option, provided that the signatory parties can be considered as adequately representative and that any person having an interest in the matter is given the opportunity to voice his objections in advance.[1] In Zambia the extension of a collective agreement may be the object of a joint request by the two parties ; if considered opportune by the Minister and subject always to the requisite publicity and consultations, such extension takes the shape of a wages regulation order.[2] In Ethiopia extension is a more authoritative measure : the law, which provides explicitly for such a possibility, does not stipulate any specific condition and therefore the Minister is free to decide both its opportuneness and its scope.[3] In some countries there is no provision for the extension of freely debated collective agreements but only for what are known as 'negotiated agreements', namely those concluded through the mediation of a conciliator after official notification of a dispute to the competent authorities.[4]

While, in the cases just mentioned, the field of application of an agreement is extended by special decision of the administration to individuals or organisations that were not represented at the negotiations, in other cases such extension stems from a permanent provision of the law. In Ghana, for instance, the application of an agreement to categories of workers not originally covered by it does not require

[1] Industrial Relations Act 1959, sections 100–101.
[2] Minimum wages, wage councils and Conditions of Employment Ordinance, section 9b.
[3] Labour Relations Decree 1962, section 3c.
[4] Tanganyika, Trade Disputes Ordinance 1962, section 35. The extension concerned refers, it would seem, both to arbitrators' awards and to the negotiated agreements that are assimilated to them.

an extension order ; but all the employers of workers who belong to the said category are *ipso facto* bound by the agreement. The same applies to Sierra Leone in respect of agreements negotiated in the joint industrial councils. In Kenya a similar solution was recently adopted : section 24 of the Trade Disputes Act 1965 lays down that any employer in a certain territorial area or section of industry may be required to observe the conditions established by the agreement in the conclusion of which a 'substantial proportion' of the employers of the said area or sector participated. The tendency to extend the field of application of collective agreements to the dimensions of that of law itself, and thus to transform the collective agreement into a kind of 'negotiated regulation', is apparently gaining ground even in countries where a liberal conception of labour relations is traditionally most in favour.

In addition to the provisions stipulated by law or agreement with a view to binding the largest possible number of employers under the terms of a collective agreement, there are certain factors apt to promote the *de facto* extension of such agreements. First, the working conditions granted by the major undertakings in a certain sector or area are very often acknowledged, in that sector or area, as having the authority of a reference or example. Secondly, when the signatory unions have a sufficiently solid organisation, they can bring pressure to bear on any of their members who would be willing to accept less favourable terms from employers who are not parties to the agreement in question. However, even when — as is the case in French-speaking countries — such pressure may take the shape of legal action against a worker who infringes the principle of trade union solidarity, it soon finds its limits in the weakness of the workers' organisations and the situation of the labour market.

## DURATION OF THE AGREEMENTS

Regarding the time factor in the application of collective agreements, in most countries the provisions of law have little weight and it is mainly the parties themselves who decide, as a rule, the date at which an agreement shall come into force, the duration of its validity, the procedures to be followed to terminate or amend it, as well as its impact on pre-existing labour relations.

As from the date of its entry into force, which may be stated in the agreement itself or, as is the rule in French-speaking countries, coincide with the deposit of a copy of the document with the clerk of the labour court, an agreement is deemed (either tacitly or on the strength of a specific provision) to abrogate previous agreements and apply not only to newly hired personnel but also to workers already employed by the undertaking or group of undertakings concerned. In most cases, however, an agreement specifically safeguards the benefits that had previously accrued individually or collectively to workers already employed at the date of its entry into force ; in fact it would generally be difficult, for reasons of social principle if not on strictly legal grounds, to cancel such benefits. The preservation of accrued benefits may be considered either as the workers' absolute right — as it is in practically all the agreements in French-speaking countries and in many of the others [1] — or as a moral or social obligation for the employer.[2] Where such a practice has become established any new agreement can, in theory, only be advantageous to the workers by granting them definitive benefits. Of course, there is always the question as to whether in practice the inclusion of well-defined wage rates in an agreement might be an insurmountable obstacle to any subsequent reduction of those rates that might be recommended as an instrument of anti-inflationary policy or for other reasons.[3]

The validity of an agreement may be of indeterminate duration — this is the case most frequently in West African countries — or limited to a specified period such as one, two or, more rarely, three years. This period, for which in some cases the law has set a minimum (one year in Ghana, three years in Ethiopia) or a maximum duration (five years in the French-speaking countries), may be shorter for the section of the agreement dealing with pay rates than for the others.[4] In practice the two systems tend to coincide. It is quite often provided that an agreement concluded for a specified period shall continue in force from year to year by tacit renewal or by a mere declaration of intent made by the parties in the months preceding

[1] For example in the Uganda motor-trade industry 1963 agreement: 'No clause of this agreement shall prejudice employees already enjoying better conditions'.
[2] The 1961 agreement signed by the Kenya National Farmers' Union stipulates that the employers-members will be 'advised in the strongest terms' not to reduce the wages of workers who are already paid at rates higher than those of the agreement.
[3] The problem might, for instance, have arisen in Dahomey in 1964, for the sector covered by collective agreements, after the Government decided to reduce the salaries of its own staff by 25 per cent.
[4] In Kenya, for instance, the agreement for minor engineering signed in 1962 was to remain in force for 12 months in respect of wages and for 2 years as regards all other conditions of employment — working hours, holidays, sickness, probation period, termination of employment.

the normal date of expiry. The duration originally specified thus becomes merely a minimum. Conversely, for agreements of indeterminate duration, the power of termination is made subject by the signatories themselves to specific formal conditions and in some cases may only be exercised after a certain time (one or two years) has elapsed. Moreover, in the event of a declaration to terminate the agreement it remains in force until the expiry of a period of notice ranging from one to three months.[1] Certain agreements, which are numerous in French-speaking Africa but occur also outside that area, e.g. in Kenya and Sudan, even provide that they shall continue in force until a new agreement is concluded. The party that takes the initiative to terminate an agreement may also be required to enclose a new draft agreement with its request.[2] Lastly, the signatories frequently undertake not to engage in strikes or lock-outs during the period of notice of termination (or review). When a minimum period of validity is fixed, whether directly or indirectly, the union sometimes explicitly undertakes not to submit or support any new claim during that period, at least with regard to matters already covered by the agreement. It should be noted, however, that a certain number of agreements contain provisions designed to ensure greater flexibility concerning the review of wage rates,[3] even when the duration originally stipulated is the same for all the clauses.

## EFFECTS AND SANCTION OF COLLECTIVE AGREEMENTS

What effects do collective agreements actually have during the period of their validity on the people they cover ? Besides setting up machinery to ease their mutual relations, the parties to an agreement have always the same aim in view : namely, to establish minimum conditions of employment which are higher than the lowest legal limits and serve in turn as minimums less than which may not be stipulated by the parties to contracts of employment. But the obligation that stems from such agreements has not everywhere the

[1] The period of notice is 6 months in many agreements in Zambia (mines, cement) and Malawi (tea plantations), 3 months in many of those concluded in the French-speaking countries.

[2] Several agreements in French-speaking Africa.

[3] Thus, several agreements in force in Nigeria or the Sudan reserve the possibility to resume talks on the clauses relating to wage rates if the economic situation should alter considerably before the date of expiry. Similarly many agreements in French-speaking countries state that claims for a review of wage rates shall not be subject to the above-mentioned conditions regarding notice.

same character and the same force.  In this respect the theoretical remarks made on the legal nature of collective agreements and the legal solutions of the problem of their sanction bring out one of the major differences — at least in the matter of principles — between the British concept, which still prevails in most English-speaking countries, and the concept which the former French territories have taken over from French law.

Under the former system a collective agreement is merely a sort of 'gentleman's agreement'.  It owes its force solely to the social ethic that promotes the fulfilment of any obligations that may have been undertaken.  Consequently, there is no question of its having the same effects as a regular contract nor, more specifically, of enforcing its provisions if necessary by taking legal action.  A contract of employment that does not conform to its terms loses none of its legal value.

Conversely, the French concept has, from the earliest days, been based on the recognition of the binding effect of collective agreements.  If their assimilation to contracts of the traditional type has sometimes been questioned, it was with a view to giving them a still greater authority than such contracts, an authority equal in practice to that of administrative regulations or even of the law itself.  Some commentators, considering more particularly the situation created by the *Code* of 1952 — a situation that has been prolonged and strengthened by subsequent developments in the French-speaking countries — have gone so far as to say that the contractual framework of a collective agreement is now no more than an 'empty shell'.[1]  Their opinion apparently coincides with that of the authors of the *Code*, for whom a collective agreement is 'the law of a trade made by its members'.  No doubt it is only when a collective agreement is the object of an extension order — which, as we have seen, is a very frequent occurrence — that it is formally recognised as having the force of a regulation.  But in every other case it has at least the specific quality of a contract.  The labour codes state that a collective agreement is automatically applicable, 'saving provisions more favourable to the workers', to the relations that stem from individual contracts, and its non-observance may give rise to a claim for damages both by the worker concerned and by the union to which he belongs.[2]

The law relating to collective agreements is clearly fundamentally

[1] Gonidec and Kirsch, *op. cit.* p. 165.
[2] Where an agreement has been extended by Ministerial Decree, an infringement of its provisions concerning wages may also give rise to criminal proceedings.

different in the two groups of countries. But the differences in the effective authority of agreements are not as great as the differences in their legal status might suggest. Experience shows that the forces of custom and social pressure may well provide a foundation of respect for the substance of the agreement as solid as that derived from the law or from a court decision. Even in French-speaking countries, as in their former mother country, it seldom happens that the formal divergence between a contract of employment and a collective agreement warrants the peremptory substitution of a clause of the agreement for the corresponding clause of the individual contract and the application of civil or penal sanctions. This goes to prove that respect for a collective agreement stems less from the coercive action of a court than from the voluntary acceptance of its recognised terms. In English-speaking countries an open refusal by employers to fulfil their obligations under collective agreements does not appear, as a rule, to be a serious problem. This willingness to observe the terms of agreements has been encouraged by the growing importance of employers' associations ; the pressure of the group, which aims at eliminating unfair competition, acts in the same direction as the moral obligation of each individual member. The difficulties that so often accompany the negotiation of an agreement and the obstinate refusal by many employers to join employers' organisations are clear evidence that the contracting parties are called upon to concede an important element of their freedom to settle the conditions of employment on their own terms. Workers who are offered less favourable conditions than those to which they are entitled — and, though it is impossible to count them, they are believed to be far from rare exceptions — are found mostly outside the field of application of collective agreements ; particularly in small agricultural and industrial undertakings whose staff as a rule are covered only by Government decisions on minimum wages. As a result there is every likelihood that violations of the law will be more frequent than violations of collective agreements, even when in principle the latter have no legal force.

None the less, many English-speaking countries — some of whom may have done so out of an authoritarian spirit no less than for practical reasons — have in the last few years abandoned their former attitude to collective bargaining and have approached the 'legalistic' position of French-speaking Africa ; this approach has been adopted entirely in some of the most recent legislation.

In Ghana, since 1958 the provisions of a collective agreement have been regarded as the terms of a contract of employment between each worker to whom the agreement applies and his employer. This very fact gives them the executory effect of such a contract.[1] In Sudan and Ethiopia too, the binding nature of a collective agreement stems from the laws governing labour-management relations.[2] In Sierra Leone agreements concluded through the joint industrial councils, once they have been published in the Official Gazette with the consent of the Labour Commissioner, become, as regards legal force and sanction (which is penal), equivalent to decisions of the Wages Boards.[3]

In other countries where collective agreements do not have *ipso facto* the force of law, they may be declared binding by the competent authorities when the parties submit a joint request to that effect. When this occurs, the provisions of the agreement in question cannot be amended or waived by individual agreements and their non-observance is an offence. This applies in Rhodesia to agreements concluded in an industrial council and in Zambia to all agreements dealing with pay rates or conditions of employment.[4]

Lastly, in several cases, particularly in Tanzania and Malawi, under the Acts or Orders on the settlement of disputes, a 'negotiated agreement' by which the parties settle amicably, with the help of a conciliator, a dispute on the establishment of conditions of employment is just as binding as an arbitrator's award.[5] In Kenya, where collective agreements are no more explicitly recognised as binding on the parties than in the two countries just mentioned, their non-observance may give rise to an appeal to the Minister ; and if the Industrial Court, to which the Minister refers the appeal, finds that the conditions of employment granted by the employer are actually less favourable than those laid down in the agreement, it must make an award requiring the employer to observe the recognised terms or conditions.[6]

Another aspect of the problem of the authority of collective agreements is the reluctance sometimes shown by the workers' organisations, particularly to observe the period fixed by an agreement during which no new claims may be entered. No doubt the comments —

[1] Industrial Relations Act, section 17.
[2] Sudanese Act of 1960, Art. 5 : Ethiopian Act of 1962, Art. 35.
[3] Wages Board Ordinance, sections 26–30.
[4] For Zambia, see section (A) of the Ordinance of Minimum Wages, Wages Boards and Conditions of Employment ; for Rhodesia, Arts. 99 and 109 of the Industrial Relations Act of 1959.
[5] For Tanzania, the Labour Disputes Act of 1962, Art. 25 ; for Malawi, Art. 22 of the Labour Disputes Act.　　　[6] Trades Disputes Act 1965, section 24

often extremely harsh — that this breach of the agreement leads many employers to make, have some justification. However, difficulties do occur and the behaviour of the unions is not always without good cause. Increases in price levels, for example, make it hard for them to continue to accept the terms of an agreement that has been concluded to cover a long period of time without any possibility of the wage levels being reviewed. When the signing of an agreement is dictated by impatience to reach a decision and is accompanied by mental reservations, misunderstandings are inevitable and they are made more frequent in Africa owing to the vast differences in culture, and in some cases by the language barrier between the parties. These factors explain in part — if they do not justify — an irresponsible attitude towards the carrying out of the terms embodied in the agreement. Moreover, a full understanding and appreciation of the significance, value and practical usefulness of a formal undertaking postulates a level of knowledge and an experience of the requirements of modern economies that not all union leaders possess in countries where the trade union movement has only recently got under way. To alleviate difficulties of this kind is the purpose of the provisions in the recent Kenyan Act under which the Minister may by order require the parties to comply with an agreement when he believes that its non-observance might lead to a strike.[1] A still more radical solution is aimed at by the increasingly numerous laws that declare illegal, in particular, those strikes which infringe on an existing collective agreement. In French-speaking countries, independently of whether such a law exists or not, the non-observance by the workers, or their organisations, of the recognised clauses (concerning, for instance, notice to strike) might, at least in theory, warrant legal action by the employer. Where no specific legislation exists some employers in English-speaking countries have included a specific clause in their collective agreements making their observance a condition of the continued recognition of the union.

## GRIEVANCES ARISING FROM THE IMPLEMENTATION OF COLLECTIVE AGREEMENTS

The authority of collective agreements is seldom questioned in principle even where it rests entirely on the free consent of the parties, and one may say that in this respect they have already reached

[1] Ibid., section 20.

a point that elsewhere demanded a slow and laborious development. But their interpretation and practical application still encounter a great many difficulties. Various methods may be and are in fact employed to overcome these difficulties.

The mass of individual disputes occasioned by the application of collective agreements — and this study is no place to enumerate them — is apparently due, more or less uniformly in the various African countries, to certain predominant causes that may be grouped under three heads.

There is the grading of the worker when hired, namely his assignment to a certain step of the wage scale in keeping with his qualifications. However, no matter how meticulously each job may be graded and specified in a collective agreement, as we have seen the determination of an individual's abilities is still a matter of estimation by the employer and consequently subject to disagreement.

The question of dismissal seems to be still more serious in the economic context of recent years when labour markets have expanded too little, if indeed they have not shrunk ; all the more so because this problem, unlike the one just mentioned, hardly lends itself to compromise solutions. Employers, aware of the gravity of the issue, have sought to safeguard their freedom of action on this point, and particularly as regards the major ground for dismissals, namely redundancy.[1] They are bound, none the less, in most cases to keep in their employ, as a matter of priority, subject to appropriate qualifications, those workers who have the greatest seniority. But the principle of 'equal pay for equal work' also presupposes a comparison of merits, and here agreement risks being all the more difficult because, generally speaking, unions and employers start out with rather divergent views as to the relative importance of the various factors to be taken into account. The unions consider that the personal status of the worker concerned (seniority, family situation) gives rise to a genuine title to employment, whereas the employers tend to insist more or less exclusively on the priority of efficiency and skill. Where, as in Mali, employers have been deprived of the right to dismiss staff, this measure has not contributed any more to the establishment of smooth worker-management relations than the restrictions on the right of workers to submit wage claims.

Lastly, the day-to-day operation of an undertaking produces the frictions that are inherent in the life of any hierarchically organised

---

[1] See on this point the developments in the chapter on the content of collective agreements.

and disciplined community. The problems raised by these frictions are not unrelated to the implementation of collective agreements, though they may not depend exclusively on it. In fact, while internal organisation and the setting up of disciplinary sanctions rest first and foremost with the employer, there are agreements, as we have seen, that give the workers' representatives a share in his authority. At times even respect for the workers' dignity — which is far from being the outcome of spontaneous evolution, as is proved by the frequent disputes that stem from disparaging remarks — is stipulated in a collective agreement.[1]

Whatever their cause, and even if they are apparently of minor importance, the very numerous disputes raised by the application and interpretation of the legal and contractual provisions covering conditions of employment constitute a serious problem. The gravity of this problem must not be underestimated, because if the disputes are not settled in time their effects are apt to be out of all proportion to their causes. In many countries it has been found that when, for the reasons mentioned above, strikes have tended to lose their value as claim-supporting weapons, sporadic and more or less spontaneous stoppages still occur relatively frequently as a display of discontent or the will to protest.

In the various parts of Africa the legal or contractual machinery for settling disputes of this kind bears the imprint of the prevailing tradition, but that does not prevent the use of similar procedures at the initial stage of a settlement — which is very often the ultimate stage as well.

The first and most generally adopted step consists in raising the grievance with the immediate superior and then approaching the next superior in the line of management. Many collective agreements in English-speaking Africa make this step the indispensable starting point of any procedure for settling an individual dispute, and fix the conditions under which it may be taken. They recognise that the worker concerned is entitled to be assisted in his dealings with the supervisor by the shop steward or, at a higher level, by the union secretary. Occasionally, too, they set a time limit within which the employer or his representative must submit his point of view on the object of the dispute.

In the French-speaking countries, where the legal codes now in

[1] For instance, the agreement of 1962 for agriculture in Somalia, after defining the workers' duties towards their superiors, adds for the latter's benefit: 'In keeping with the workers' professional dignity, superiors shall imbue their relations with their subordinates with a spirit of collaboration and a sense of urbanity'.

force follow their French exemplar and do not in principle recognise trade-union representation at the plant level, the task of raising with the employer individual or collective grievances regarding terms of service, and particularly the application of collective agreements, is entrusted to *délégués du personnel* elected by all the workers on the payroll of the undertaking. These latter retain, however, the right to assert their grievances or, if necessary, to have them supported by the representative of their union. The employer is obliged to receive the staff delegates at regular intervals and, when an urgent case arises, at their request. They are entitled to receive a written reply if they believe that this would be to their advantage.

Free discussion between the parties concerned — whether or not it is explicitly laid down by the law or a collective agreement — without the interference of persons unconnected with the undertaking seems capable, in the African context more perhaps than anywhere else, of giving great assistance in settling disputes that stem from day-to-day labour relations. But where it most readily takes root — namely, in African undertakings — there is a danger that its effects may be restricted by the over-personalisation of employer-worker relations, while elsewhere its development may be impeded by the rigidity of those relations and the strengthening of the principle of authority. Hence the advantage of having, at an early stage, a third party who offers adequate assurance of impartiality and competence. Thanks to these qualities and the prestige due to their position, the officials of the Labour Ministry seem as a rule very well placed to fill that role, which entails the duties of counsellor no less than those of conciliator.

In the French-speaking countries the law gives the labour inspectors the right to act as conciliators in all disputes between a worker and his employer. They discharged this duty during the lengthy period when they alone were entrusted with it, with a success that is generally considered quite remarkable — at least in respect of the great mass of African workers for whom an appeal to the civil courts (which was their only resort before the establishment of the labour courts) was practically out of the question because of the slowness and cost of legal action. Since 1952 they have continued to make their good offices available for the amicable settlement of disputes and both employers and workers may resort to them before applying to the labour courts set up by the *Code*. Even today that is still one of their essential duties.

In other countries, even where the intervention of Labour Ministry officials, which is quite informal at this stage, has no legal sanction, it is no less successful in meeting the needs and expectations of a great many people. In some cases, indeed — either because no machinery has been agreed upon or because recourse to that machinery presupposes on the part of the trade union an initiative that it is ill prepared to deploy — their intervention has apparently become the prevalent method for settling all individual disputes.[1]

Whatever their intrinsic advantages and their efficiency, the methods just described are not always adequate, particularly when there is a question of a worker keeping or losing his job. The methods subsequently employed differ considerably in the two groups of countries we are studying, though scrutiny of them shows that they have some features in common because their situations and problems are to a certain extent similar.

In most English-speaking countries, where collective agreements as a rule contain a more or less detailed description of these methods, the last stage of the procedure is sometimes the joint investigation of individual grievances by the competent union delegate and the management of the undertaking. And the procedure is closed, in principle, by a decision by the management which is notified to the union in the days following the exchange of views. In other cases — and they are the majority — the raising of a grievance at the successive levels of the line of management is also the normal way to settle grievances arising from a breach, real or alleged, of existing terms of service. When, however, this does not lead to a result satisfactory to the complainant, a conflict of rights, even though individual, may follow the course normally laid down for claims for an alteration to terms of employment. This involves their investigation first by a joint plant or estate committee ; then, if necessary by a joint industrial council whose membership includes a fixed proportion of the unions represented in the undertaking concerned ; and lastly, if these steps are unsuccessful, resort to procedures established by the Trades Disputes Acts (official report to the competent authorities, conciliation, arbitration). These latter are always considered as a last resort both by the collective agreements and by the Acts, which lay down as a rule that the Minister's representative shall start out by making sure that the machinery established by agreement between the parties has been fully utilised.[2] Quite often, if a grievance arising from a

---

[1] Thus in 1963, in the Tanga district of Tanzania, where such disputes were very numerous (1577 in the first six months of the year), 97 per cent were settled by the labour services without any formal procedure.

[2] It should be noted that the various Trades Disputes Acts, including those that

K

breach, real or alleged, of the existing terms of service concerns a group of workers or raises a question of principle and is, therefore, apt to set a precedent, it is equated to a claim for the review of terms of service and brought right away before the joint conciliatory bodies at plant or industry level. Finally, in some cases grievances not settled by direct agreement between union and management are brought immediately before the Labour Department (and not before the joint bodies mentioned above), as laid down in the Trades Disputes Acts currently in force. Summing up, and greatly simplifying a situation utterly diverse in detail though fairly uniform in its main lines, one may perhaps say that there is only one procedure for settling all labour disputes, but that for disputes of a certain importance it is set in motion at a stage which is only reached by minor disputes when attempts to settle them at earlier stages have failed.

The system in force in French-speaking countries is apparently rather far removed from this concept. Not only does the law play the leading role, but a far clearer difference is drawn, in the matter of procedure, between individual and collective disputes.[1] Only the latter — which may concern either the application of an existing agreement or the stipulation of new terms of service — can be settled by the methods of conciliation and arbitration mentioned above.[2] The great majority of disputes concerning the application of agreements are of the individual type and — once the labour inspectors fail to settle them — come under the exclusive jurisdiction of the labour courts. These courts are formed by a magistrate and an equal number (two in the 1952 *Code*, only one in the most recent codes) of employers' and workers' assessors selected from lists drawn up by the most representative organisations of the two parties. Their decisions are final in disputes of minor importance but in other cases are subject to appeal to the ordinary courts of law. The first stage of this procedure, which is free throughout, is an attempt at conciliation *in camera*. The whole procedure takes place in the presence of

stipulate the compulsory intervention of a court of arbitration as a last resort, do not as a rule distinguish between different kinds of labour disputes.

[1] Lacking any statutory definition, the courts consider that collective disputes are those which involve a group of workers and, even if they stem from a decision concerning a single worker, overstep the latter's personal interest owing to the matter at stake ; an example is dismissal justified by trade union activity (Gonidec *et* Kirsch, *op. cit.* p. 376). The Guinean Code of 1960 alone defines a collective dispute as any dispute between an employer and at least 10 of the wage earners or salaried workers on his payroll, with the proviso that this number must comprise at least one-quarter of the workers in the undertaking or plant or that the dispute risks causing a strike. [2] Cf. Chapter 4.

the parties, who may also be represented or assisted, not only by a lawyer but even by a worker or employer in the same sector, or by a representative of a workers' or employers' organisation. Indeed, the representation of workers before these courts is an important aspect of trade-union activity and undoubtedly one of its most tangible manifestations at a time when claims for better conditions encounter obstacles that are not easily overcome. In the new codes in French-speaking Africa this system is maintained more or less as laid down in the law of 1952 except for secondary arrangements aimed at simplifying or speeding up its operation.

Experience has shown that the results obtained by the labour courts were successful enough to justify the perpetuation of the system in recent legislation. As a rule, however, the parties to collective agreements have found it advisable to supplement them with machinery that may be utilised in connection with two special types of disputes.

The first are disputes arising out of the interpretation of the agreements. Many of these provide that such disputes shall be brought before an *ad hoc* committee formed by representatives of each of the signatory organisations and convened at the request of one of the parties. But in practice this procedure loses much of its significance due to the rule that all decisions must be unanimous.

Far more important and efficient in practice is the action of the joint classification committees, set up by most collective agreements in French-speaking Africa, to decide on all disputes concerning job grading after a claim raised directly with the employer has proved fruitless and before resorting to the labour court. They associate, under the chairmanship of the labour inspector, two workers' and two employers' representatives, who may co-opt as experts one or two of their colleagues specially qualified to judge the dispute. These bodies are in close contact with the actual situation of the undertaking and are obliged, by the clauses under which they are set up, to act quickly. As a result, thanks to their success in discharging their duties, they have been able to lighten very substantially the burden on the labour courts. Such a system which operates in one of the fields where disputes most commonly arise, closely resembles the conciliatory procedures adopted by the English-speaking countries. If we want to compare in more general terms the prevailing machinery in each group of countries, we must not lose sight of the place reserved in the composition of the labour courts for the representatives of the workers' and employers' organisations or, in their operation, of the obligation to start by an attempt at conciliation ; as well as of the parties' right to be assisted or represented by a member of the employers' organisation or a trade-union official.

Whatever the basis — legal or contractual — of the procedure for settling disputes and the formal framework within which it functions, the close association of workers' and employers' representatives in the operation of that procedure, and the scope left in its many successive stages for reaching an amicable settlement, are intrinsic features of the African systems of industrial relations. If these features meet a need generally felt — to a varying degree — in all types of industrial organisation, one is justified in assuming that they fit extremely well in a social context where by tradition the solution of differences has always been sought rather in discussion and compromise than in forceful coercion.[1]

---

[1] See on this point the article on 'The Evolution of Labour Disputes Settlement Procedures in Certain African Countries' in the *International Labour Review* of February 1965.

Appendix I

# KENYA
# INDUSTRIAL RELATIONS CHARTER

NAIROBI

*15th October 1962*

PREAMBLE

The Government of Kenya, the Federation of Kenya Employers and the Kenya Federation of Labour :

1. Considering that at their Conference held in Nairobi on Tuesday, the 3rd, and Thursday, the 5th July, 1962, convened by and under the Chairmanship of the Minister of Labour, The Hon. T. J. Mboya, M.L.C., agreed to endeavour to prepare an Industrial Relations Charter ;

2. Realising that it is in the National interest for the Government, Management and Workers to recognise that consultation and co-operation on a basis of mutual understanding render an essential contribution to the efficiency and productivity of an undertaking and that progress can only be made on a foundation of good terms and conditions of employment which include security of service and income, also the improvement of Workers' conditions of service ;

3. Desiring to make the greatest possible contribution to the success and prosperity of Kenya ;

agree upon the following Charter of Industrial Relations.

1. *Agreed Responsibilities of Management and Unions*

   (i) that the existing machinery for settlement of disputes should be utilised as quickly as possible ;

   (ii) that both sides undertake to settle any or all industrial disputes at the appropriate level and according to the procedure laid down hereafter ;

   (iii) that affirming their faith in democratic principles, they agree to settle all future differences, disputes and grievances by mutual negotiation, conciliation and voluntary arbitration or strikes or lock-outs as a last resort ;

   (iv) that there should be no strike or lock-out without notice ;

(v) that neither party will have recourse to intimidation or victimisation or conduct contrary to the spirit of this Charter ;

(vi) that they undertake to promote maximum co-operation in the interests of good industrial relations between their representatives at all levels and abide by the spirit of agreements mutually entered into ;

(vii) that they undertake to observe strictly the grievance procedure outlined in the Recognition Agreement which will ensure a speedy and full investigation to settlement ;

(viii) that they will educate the Management Personnel and Employees regarding their obligations to each other for the purpose of good industrial relations ;

(ix) that they respect each other's right to freedom of association ;

(x) that they will deal promptly with all correspondence that arises between them.

### 2. *Management Agree*

(i) to recognise the Union appropriate to its particular industry and to accord reasonable facilities for the normal functioning of the Union in the undertaking ;

(ii) to discourage such practices as (a) interference with the rights of employees to enrol or continue as Union members (b) discrimination, restraint or coercion against any employee because of recognised activity of trade unions (c) victimisation of any employee and abuse of authority in any form (d) abusive or intemperate language ; and (e) generally to respect the provision of the I.L.O. Convention No. 98 ;

(iii) to take action for (a) settlement of grievances and (b) implementation of settlements, awards, decisions and orders, as speedily as possible ;

(iv) in cases of misconduct to distinguish between misdemeanours justifying immediate dismissal and those where discharge must be preceded by a warning, reprimand, suspension or some other form of disciplinary action and to arrange that all such disciplinary action should be subject to appeal ;

(v) that every employee has the right to approach Management on personal problems and agree always to make accredited representatives available to listen to the day-to-day problems of employees ;

(vi) to impress upon their staffs the contents of this Charter and to take appropriate action where Management inquiries reveal that the spirit or contents of this Charter have been contravened and to give full publicity on their Notice Boards to this Charter ;

(vii) to discourage any breach of the peace or civil commotion by Employers or their Agents.

## Appendix I

### 3. Union(s) Agree

(i) not to engage in any activities which are contrary to the spirit of this Charter;

(ii) to discourage any breach of the peace or civil commotion by Union members;

(iii) that their members will not engage or cause other employees to engage in any Union activity during working hours, unless as provided for by law or by agreement;

(iv) to discourage such practices as (a) negligence of duty (b) careless operation (c) damage to property (d) interference with or disturbance to normal work (e) insubordination (f) abusive or intemperate language, and generally to respect the provisions of I.L.O. Convention No. 98;

(v) to take action to implement awards, agreements, settlements and decisions as speedily as possible;

(vi) that where strike or lock-out action occurs essential services (the cessation of which would cause injury to humans or animals) shall be maintained, but the employees concerned shall not be called upon to perform any other duties than the maintenance of the service concerned;

(vii) to display in conspicuous places in the Union offices the provisions of this Code and to impress upon their officers and members the contents of this Charter and to take appropriate action where Union inquiries reveal that the spirit or contents of this Charter have been contravened.

## RECOGNITION

It is agreed in principle that the Model Recognition Agreement as appendix 'A'* is hereby accepted as a guide to parties in all future agreements and that the following principles should apply:

(i) that provision by the Registrar of Trade Unions to F.K.E. or to the employer of a certificate that the Union is properly registered and exists effectively to represent the particular employees should decide the question of recognition and negotiations should then commence based on the Model Recognition Agreement and for the eventual setting up of Joint Machinery as may be appropriate to the particular Industry or undertaking;

(ii) that minor breaches of agreements by either party shall not give justification for withdrawing recognition but shall be processed as ' disputes';

(iii) that these principles be brought to the notice of parties who are not affiliated to F.K.E. or K.F.L.

* The model Recognition Agreement is subject to many variations, and appendix 'A' is therefore not included.

## JOINT K.F.L./F.K.E. DISPUTES COMMISSIONS

Machinery exists at industrial level as provided for in the Recognition Agreement for dealing with disputes that may arise from time to time, firstly through the local or district negotiating committee or through the Joint Industrial Councils. That machinery is not intended to be super-seded in any way by the procedure of the Joint Disputes Commissions, and it is agreed that both sides will wherever possible endeavour to settle dis-putes, using the machinery provided in the negotiated agreements.

The specific object of the Joint Disputes Commissions is to prevent disputes involving loss of time and money to all concerned, and to deal immediately and effectively with disagreements, in order to prevent any unnecessary stoppage of work. The use of the Commissions is entirely voluntary and is not intended to prevent parties who so wish utilising the processes provided under the terms of the Trade Disputes (Arbitration and Inquiry) Ordinance.

It is agreed that, on receipt of recommendations from a Joint Disputes Commission, both parties to the dispute should indicate acceptance or rejection of the Commission's recommendations on the matters referred to it, within a period of seven days from the date of receipt of the Com-mission's report or such longer period as the Commission shall decide.

## REDUNDANCY

In the event of redundancy, the following principles will apply :

(i) the Union concerned shall be informed of the reasons for and the extent of intended redundancy ;

(ii) the principle should be adopted of 'Last in, First out' in the par-ticular category of employees affected subject to all other factors such as skill, relative merit, ability and reliability being equal ;

(iii) the redundant employee will be entitled to the appropriate period of notice or pay in lieu. The principle of severance pay is agreed but the form and amount of such pay shall be subject to joint negotiation.

## EMPLOYMENT POLICY

The provisions of the I.L.O. Convention adopted June, 1962, Article 14, shall apply as follows :

1. It shall be an aim of policy to abolish all discrimination among workers on grounds of race, colour, sex, belief, tribal association or trade union affiliation in respect of :

(*a*) labour legislation and agreements which shall afford equitable economic treatment to all those lawfully resident or working in the country ;

(b) admission to public or private employment ;
(c) conditions of engagement and promotion ;
(d) opportunities for vocational training ;
(e) conditions of work ;
(f) health, safety and welfare measures ;
(g) discipline ;
(h) participation in the negotiation of collective agreements ;
(i) wages rates, which shall be fixed according to the principle of equal pay for work of equal value in the same operation and undertaking.

2. All practicable measures shall be taken to abolish, by raising the rates applicable to the lower-paid workers, any existing differences in wages rates due to discrimination by reason of race, colour, sex, belief, tribal association or trade union affiliation.

3. Workers from one country engaged for employment in another country may be granted, in addition to their wages, benefits in cash or in kind to meet any reasonable personal or family expenses resulting from employment away from their homes. This is to apply in cases of special skills not available locally.

4. The foregoing provisions of this Article shall be without prejudice to such measures as the competent authority may think it necessary or desirable to take for the safeguarding of motherhood and for ensuring the health, safety and welfare of women workers.

## STRIKES AND LOCK-OUTS

It is agreed that in future the Federation of Kenya Employers on the one hand, and the Kenya Federation of Labour, on the other hand, shall discourage and seek to bring to an end any strike or lock-out which may arise from or be caused by any question, difference or dispute, contention, grievance or complaint with respect to work, wages or any other matter, unless and until the following steps have been taken and these have failed to settle such question of difference, etc.,

(i) the matter in dispute shall first of all be considered by the appropriate machinery as set out in the Recognition Agreement ;
(ii) failing settlement at Joint Industrial Council, such dispute shall be reported forthwith by the parties concerned therein to their representative National Officials and be immediately jointly dealt with by them either by invoking Joint Disputes Commission procedure or by reference to the Chief Labour Officer.

## INTIMIDATION

It is hereby agreed that employees and management shall enjoy adequate protection against any acts of interference by each other or each other's agents or members. Such protection shall apply more particularly in respect of such acts as :

(*a*) will make the employment of an individual employee subject to the condition that he shall or shall not join a union ;

(*b*) the dismissal of an employee by reason of union membership or acts of participation in union activities outside working hours or with the consent of the employer within working hours ;

(*c*) the drawing up, issuing or publication of discriminatory lists or any action which will prevent a supervisor or shop steward from carrying out his normal functions.

## JOINT CONSULTATION

Management and employees recognise that consultation and co-operation on the basis of mutual confidence render an essential contribution to the efficiency and productivity of an undertaking and also contributes to the social and economic well-being of all.

It is therefore agreed that :

(i) full support will be given by both parties to the constitution and the regulations of the National Joint Consultative Council and to all other freely negotiated joint machinery set up under the Recognition Agreement in the various industries throughout Kenya ;

(ii) encouragement shall be given to voluntary agreements between the parties ;

(iii) management shall take appropriate measures to facilitate the proper functioning of joint machinery by making available facilities for meetings and, in appropriate cases, the staff essential thereto. It shall also allow representatives of the employees the necessary time within reason to attend such meetings without loss of pay ;

(iv) it is clearly understood, however, that the employees' representatives, not being full-time paid officials of the union, are first and foremost employees of industry and as such their first and prime responsibility is to carry out the duties assigned to them as employees of their employer Company during working hours ;

(v) (*a*) that means should by readily available whereby any questions which may arise, affecting all employees or any category of employees, covered by the Agreement can be fully and promptly considered with a view to a satisfactory settlement ;

(*b*) that the recognised procedure covering negotiations and dis-

*Appendix I*

cussions between both parties should be so far as is practicable fully known and understood by the employees and by all members of Management ;

(c) that an essential factor in successful negotiations and discussions is the clear statement or report of the issues involved and of the resulting decision after mutual agreement between the parties.

## PRESS STATEMENTS

That during negotiations the Kenya Federation of Labour and the Federation of Kenya Employers agree to recommend to their affiliates that statements to the Press and the Kenya Broadcasting Corporation should be jointly made although the right of either party to communicate individually is accepted.

The Federations will also recommend that letters be not normally copied to the Press or to the Ministry of Labour.

## CONCLUSION

Both the Federation of Kenya Employers and the Kenya Federation of Labour agree to observe and abide by this Charter of Industrial Relations.

SIGNED :

Sir Colin Campbell
for and on behalf of the Federation of Kenya Employers.


P. F. Kibisu
for and on behalf of the Kenya Federation of Labour.


T. J. Mboya
Minister for Labour

137

Appendix II

# EXTRACTS FROM THE LABOUR CODE, REPUBLIC OF SENEGAL

*Act No. 61–34 to establish a Labour Code*
*Dated 15 June 1961*

## PART III

### CHAPTER IV. COLLECTIVE AGREEMENTS

*Division I.  Nature and Validity of the Agreement*

79.  A collective agreement is an agreement on conditions of employment between the representatives of one or more trade unions or organisations of workers, of the one part, and one or more trade associations or any other organisation of employers or one or more employers individually, of the other part.

A collective agreement may contain provisions which are more favourable to the workers than those of the Acts and regulations in force.  It shall not be capable of modifying any provision in such Acts and regulations which relates to matters of public policy.

Collective agreements shall define their scope.  This may be national, regional or local.

80.  The representatives of the trade unions or other organisations referred to in the preceding section may contract on behalf of the organisation which they represent in virtue of —

provisions in the bye-laws of the organisation ;
or a special resolution of the organisation ;
or a special authorisation in writing given to them individually by the
    organisation as a whole.

In default of the above, a collective agreement shall not be valid unless it is ratified by a special decision of the organisation.

The organisation shall themselves define their rules of procedure.

81.  A collective agreement may be of unspecified duration or of a specified duration.  Where it is made for a specified duration, this shall not exceed five years.

In the absence of any stipulation to the contrary, an agreement of a specified duration shall continue to have effect on the expiry of the agreed period as if it were an agreement of unspecified duration.

A collective agreement of unspecified duration may cease at the will of any of the parties.

Every collective agreement shall specify the procedure by which and the time at which it may be terminated, renewed or revised. It shall include a provision respecting the period of notice required for termination.

Any trade union or employer not a party to the collective agreement may become a party to it subsequently.

82. No collective agreement shall be valid unless it is made in the French language. The Council of Ministers shall issue decrees prescribing rules for the registration, publication and translation of collective agreements and the procedure for becoming a party to an existing agreement under the last paragraph of the preceding section.

Save as otherwise stipulated, a collective agreement shall be binding from the day following registration in the manner and place indicated in the above-mentioned decrees.

83. Every person who has signed a collective agreement or is a member of a signatory organisation shall be bound by the agreement. The agreement shall likewise be binding on any organisation which subsequently becomes a party to the agreement and on every person who at any time joins such an organisation.

Whenever an employer is bound by the terms of a collective agreement, the said terms shall apply to the contracts of employment made by him.

In every establishment falling within the scope of a collective agreement the terms of the agreement shall have binding force, for all workers of the establishment, in the relations created by individual contracts of employment, unless there are provisions more favourable to the workers.

*Division II. Collective Agreements Capable of being Extended and Procedure for Extension*

84. If so requested by one of the organisations deemed to be most representative of the employers or workers concerned, or on his own initiative, the Minister of Labour and Social Security shall arrange for a joint committee to meet with a view to concluding a collective agreement to regulate relations between employers and workers in a particular branch of activity on a national, regional or local basis.

The Minister of Labour and Social Security shall by order prescribe the composition of the said joint committee, which shall include representatives in equal number of the most representative workers' organisations and of the most representative employers' organisations or, in default thereof, of the employers.

Subsidiary agreements may be concluded for each of the principal occupational groups; they shall contain the particular terms of employment for the said groups, and shall be negotiated by the representatives of the most representative organisations for the groups in question.

The extent to which a trade union or other organisation is representative shall be determined by the Minister of Labour and Social Security after assembling all relevant information and consulting the labour and social security services concerned.

The relevant information shall include data on—

membership and the results of elections of staff representatives;
independence;
contributions;
the experience and the type and degree of activity of the association.

Appeal against the Minister's decision may be made to the Head of the Government within 15 days.

The file furnished by the Minister of Labour and Social Security shall contain all the relevant information obtained and the opinion of the labour and social security services.

The foregoing provisions shall not be interpreted as authorising the administration to inspect the membership registers and treasurer's books of the trade union.

If a joint committee is unable to overcome a difference of opinion regarding one or more provisions to be inserted in a collective agreement, the Inspectorate of Labour and Social Security shall, at the request of any of the parties, assist in overcoming this difference of opinion.

85. The collective agreements referred to in this division shall contain provisions regarding:

(1) freedom of association and freedom of opinion for the workers;
(2) the scale of indices applicable to the inter-occupational guaranteed minimum wage to obtain the minimum wages corresponding to the various degrees of occupational skill in the branch of activity concerned;
(3) the rules governing overtime and the rates payable for overtime worked during the day or at night on working days or on Sundays or public holidays;
(4) the duration of engagements for a trial period and of the period of notice;
(5) staff representatives;
(6) the rules for revising, amending or terminating all or part of the collective agreement;
(7) the method of applying the principle 'equal pay for equal work' in respect of women and young persons;
(8) paid leave;

(9) travel allowances ;
(10) (where appropriate) expatriation allowances ;
(11) the class of ticket and weight of luggage for the worker and his family, where the worker is travelling from his habitual place of residence to his place of employment or vice versa or where the place of employment happens to be changed.

They may also contain *inter alia* provisions concerning :

(1) service, attendance and output bonuses ;
(2) allowances for occasional expenses connected with the work, or equivalent disbursements ; transport allowances ;
(3) luncheon or other meal bonuses for workers who have to eat their meal at the workplace ;
(4) general rules for payment by results or on a commission basis where this method of remuneration is deemed to be wholly or partly feasible ;
(5) extra pay for arduous, dangerous, unhealthy or dirty work ;
(6) rules for engagement and dimissal of workers (so, however, that the workers' free choice of trade union is not impaired) ;
(7) (where appropriate) arrangements for apprenticeship and vocational training in the branch of activity under consideration ;
(8) the special conditions of employment for women and young persons in certain undertakings covered by the agreement ;
(9) (where appropriate) the mode of providing the security deposit referred to in Chapter VI of this Part ;
(10) the part-time employment of certain categories of personnel and their rates of remuneration ;
(11) the organisation, management and financing of welfare and medical services ;
(12) special working conditions (shift work, work on the weekly rest day and work on public holidays) ;
(13) the agreed arbitration machinery by which any collective labour dispute arising between employers and workers bound by the agreement shall or may be settled.

The conditions in which non-compulsory provisions that have proved to be useful may be declared compulsory shall be prescribed by decree.

86. Whenever a collective agreement concerning a given branch of activity has been made at the national or regional level, the collective agreements made at lower levels (regional or local) shall adapt the said agreement or certain of its provisions to the particular conditions of employment at the lower level.

The lower-level agreements may include additional provisions and clauses more favourable to the workers.

87. At the request of one of the most representative organisations or on

the initiative of the Minister of Labour and Social Security, the provisions of all collective agreements conforming to the rules given in this Division may, by an order made jointly by the Minister of Labour and Social Security and the Minister of Finance, be made compulsory for all employers and workers in the area and trades covered by the agreement.

Such an extension of the effects and sanctions of the collective agreement shall be made for such a period and on such conditions as are laid down in the agreement, except that, in the absence of any provision to the contrary, it shall not be retroactive :

Provided that any provisions which are contrary to the existing legislative or administrative enactments shall be excluded from the extension by the Minister of Labour and Social Security after receiving the recommendations (with reasons) of the National Advisory Council for Labour and Social Security. He may also, in like manner, exclude from the agreement, without altering its general effect any clauses which are inappropriate to the situation in the branch of activity in the area under consideration.

88. A ministerial order under the preceding section shall cease to have effect when the collective agreement has ceased to operate between the parties as a result of its termination or non-renewal.

On the proposal of the Minister of Labour and Social Security, after the recommendations (with reasons) of the National Advisory Council for Labour and Social Security have been received, a ministerial order under the preceding section may be revoked for the purpose of terminating the extension of the collective agreement or certain of its provisions, whenever it appears that the agreement or the provisions in question no longer correspond to the situation in the branch of activity in the area under consideration.

89. In the absence of any collective agreement or pending the conclusion of such an agreement under the rules given in this Division, the Minister of Labour and Social Security may, by an order made after receipt of the recommendations of the National Advisory Council for Labour and Social Security, regulate conditions of employment in a given trade or profession by following the general lines of collective agreements that may exist in other States or of accepted international standards.

Such an order may be made for a given trade or profession or for a group of trades or professions in which conditions of employment are comparable. It may rescind collective agreements made before the present Code and remaining in force (with the exception of those provisions which conflict with this Act) pending the establishment of new agreements under this Act.

In the absence of any collective agreement or pending the conclusion of such an agreement, conditions of employment in trades or professions followed in public establishments or services shall be regulated by decree.

90. No order extending or revoking the extension of an agreement shall

be made without prior consultation of the organisations and all persons concerned, which and who shall submit their comments within thirty days.

The procedure for such consultation shall be prescribed by order of the Minister of Labour and Social Security.

An order extending wages shall be exempt from the requirements of prior consultation.

### Division III. *Agreements for Specific Establishments*

91. Agreements relating to one or more than one specific establishment may be made between an employer or a group of employers and representatives of the most representative trade unions of the staff of the establishment or establishments concerned actually employed therein.

The object of such agreements shall be to adapt to particular conditions in the establishment or establishments concerned the provisions of national, regional or local collective agreements and the orders provided for in section 89 and in particular the rules for awarding and calculating pay by results, bonuses based on individual and group output, and productivity bonuses.

They may include new provisions and clauses which are more favourable to the workers.

Where there are no national, regional or local collective agreements or orders as prescribed in section 89, agreements for specific establishments shall deal only with the fixing of wages and wage supplements, except in cases where exemptions are made by the Minister of Labour and Social Security.

The provisions of sections 81, 82 and 83 shall apply to agreements covered by this section.

### Division IV. *Collective Agreements in Public Services, Undertakings and Establishments*

92. Where the staff of public services, undertakings and establishments is not covered by special rules, prescribed by laws or regulations, collective agreements may be made in accordance with the provisions of this chapter.

A list of public services, undertakings and establishments employing staff covered by such special rules shall be issued by decree.

93. Whenever a collective agreement is extended by an order made under section 87, it shall, unless otherwise provided, also apply to any public services, undertakings and establishments covered by this Division which, by reason of their nature and activity, fall within the scope of such agreement.

### Division V. *Fulfilment of the Agreement*

94. The workers' and employers' organisations which are bound by a collective agreement or by an agreement of the type mentioned in section 91 above shall abstain from doing anything likely to impair the due

fulfilment of the agreement. They shall be answerable for such fulfilment only to the extent laid down in the agreement.

95. Organisation capable of suing and being sued which are bound by a collective agreement or an agreement of the type mentioned in section 91 above may bring an action for damages in their own name against any other organisations, against their own members or against any persons bound by the agreement, which or who have violated their contractual obligations.

96. The persons bound by a collective agreement or by an agreement of the type mentioned in section 91 above may bring an action for damages against other persons or organisations bound by the agreement who or which have violated their contractual obligations.

97. Organisations capable of suing and being sued which are bound by a collective agreement or by an agreement of the type mentioned in section 91 above may bring any action founded upon the agreement on behalf of their members, without being required to prove that they have special authority from the member concerned, on condition that the said member has received notice of the intention without making an objection. The member concerned may intervene at any time in the proceedings instituted by the organisation.

Where an action founded upon an agreement is brought by a person or by an organisation, any organisation capable of suing and being sued whose members are bound by the said agreement may intervene at any time in the proceedings in virtue of the collective interest of its members in the settlement of the dispute.

### Division VI. Transitional Provisions

98. Collective agreements made before the present Act shall remain in force, with the exception of those provisions which are contrary to it. These collective agreements may be the subject of extension orders as provided by this Act in the chapter on collective agreements. If they have been the subject of extension orders made before this Act, these extension orders shall remain in force so far as they do not conflict with its provisions.

. . . . .

## PART VIII. LABOUR DISPUTES

200. Individual and collective labour disputes shall be dealt with according to the procedure laid down in this Part.

### CHAPTER I. INDIVIDUAL DISPUTES

201. The labour courts shall hear individual disputes between workers and their employers arising out of the work relationship or in connection

with contracts of apprenticeship, collective agreements, conditions of work, health and safety and the social security scheme.

Their competence shall likewise cover disputes between the workers themselves or between employers concerning the work, and disputes between the compulsory social security institutions and their beneficiaries or members with respect to the administration of the social security scheme.

Their competence shall also include actions for the recovery of money, brought by contractors against subcontractors in the cases prescribed in section 76 above.

The competence of the labour courts shall remain unaffected even in cases where a public body or establishment is involved ; they shall be entitled to decide such cases without the parties being obliged to observe the formalities (where such exist) which have to be complied with before legal action can be taken against such public bodies or establishments.

202. The competent court shall be that for the place of employment :

Provided that in the case of litigation arising out of termination of the contract of employment and notwithstanding any agreement as to jurisdiction in the collective agreement, a worker who is normally resident in Senegal in a place other than the place in which he is employed, shall be entitled to choose between the court for his place of residence and the court for his place of employment.

203. The labour courts shall be established by a decree made on a joint recommendation of the Minister of Justice and the Minister of Labour and Social Security.

The decree shall prescribe the place where each court is to be situated, its territorial jurisdiction and its division into occupational sections where the structure of the labour market justifies this procedure.

204. The labour courts shall for administrative purposes be under the Minister of Justice.

205. Each labour court shall be composed of the following :

(1) a judge appointed by the Minister of Justice, president.

As an exceptional measure, if it is impossible to appoint a judge, or when the judge is absent, on leave or unable to attend, an official appointed by joint order of the Keeper of the Seals, Minister of Justice, and the Minister of Labour and Social Security, may act as president ;

(2) two employer assessors and two worker assessors chosen from lists drawn up in accordance with provisions of section 206 below ; for each case heard the president shall in so far as possible appoint employer assessors and worker assessors belonging to the category involved.

The regular assessors shall be replaced when they are unable to attend by substitute assessors, of whom there shall be a number equal to the number of regular assessors.

If one of the assessors is not present, the youngest member in the majority group shall not sit.

An administrative official appointed by the joint order of the Keeper of the Seals, Minister of Justice, and the Minister of Labour and Social Security shall be attached to the court as secretary.

206. The assessors and their substitutes shall be appointed by order of the Minister of Labour and Social Security on a recommendation of the Director-general of Labour and Social Security. They shall be chosen from lists submitted by the most representative trade union organisations (or, where there are no such organisations, by the inspectors of labour and social security), each list containing twice as many names as there are posts to be filled.

The assessors and there substitutes shall be appointed for one year at a time ; they may be reappointed.

The assessors and their substitutes must show that they are in possession of their civil rights and that they have not been sentenced to any of the penalties which, under the electoral laws in force, would result in being struck off the list of electors.

Assessors who do not fulfil these conditions shall cease to hold office.

. . . . .

210. Proceedings in the labour courts shall be free of charge.

For the execution of judgments in their favour workers shall be entitled to free legal aid ; when the judgment is enforceable and the worker who has won his case cannot obtain execution of the court's decision without judicial enforcement, he shall apply to the president to have the executory formula entered on the copy which has been delivered to him and charge an officer of the court with its execution.

211. Any worker or any employer may make a request in writing to the inspector of labour and social security or to his deputy or lawful substitute to bring about an amicable settlement of the dispute.

Such request shall suspend the prescriptive period referred to in section 125 of this Act as from the date of its reception by the competent inspector of labour and social security. The suspension shall remain in effect until the date of the written report terminating the attempt at conciliation at the Inspectorate of Labour and Social Security.

The inspector shall ascertain whether the parties are ready to accept conciliation on the basis of the standards set by laws, regulations or collective agreements and the individual contract.

In the case of conciliation the executory formula shall be entered by order of the president of the labour court, at the request of either party, on the conciliation report drawn up by the inspector of labour and social security, his deputy or lawful substitute.

The execution shall be carried out in the same way as in the case of a judgment of the labour court.

The competent labour court president shall be the president of the labour court within whose jurisdiction the report of conciliation was signed.

212. Where an attempt at conciliation has failed, or where no such attempt has been made, court proceedings shall be commenced by a written declaration made to the secretary of the labour court. The case shall be entered in a register specially kept for this purpose and an extract of such registration shall be delivered to the party commencing the court proceedings.

The regional inspector of labour and social security who attempted unsuccessfully to bring about the conciliation in the manner prescribed in the first two paragraphs of the previous section may, at the request of one of the parties, transmit for information to the president of the labour court hearing the case the entire file by the inspector of labour and social security on the case.

The file may also be transmitted at the request of the labour court hearing the case.

.    .    .    .    .

## CHAPTER II.  COLLECTIVE DISPUTES

231. The provisions of this Chapter shall apply to collective disputes involving the workers defined in section 1 of this Code; they shall not apply to wage earners in public services, undertakings and establishments unless there are no provisions of laws or regulations to the contrary.

### *Division I.  Conciliation*

232. Notice of every collective dispute shall be given immediately by the parties—

(1) to the inspector of labour and social security, where the dispute is limited to the territory of a regional inspectorate of labour and social security ;

(2) to the Minister of Labour and Social Security where the dispute involves the territory of two or more regional inspectorates of labour and social security.

233. The conciliation procedure shall be that provided by the collective agreement for the settlement of collective disputes.

Failure of the attempt at conciliation shall be reported without delay to the competent authority as defined in the previous section.

234. If the conciliation procedure provided for in the collective agreement is unsuccessful or if no such procedure has been attempted, an

attempt at conciliation shall be automatically made.

The regional inspector of labour and social security shall normally be competent to attempt to bring about conciliation in the case of collective disputes limited to his territorial competence : Provided that the Minister of Labour and Social Security may, particularly if the number of disputes justifies such action, appoint by order an inspector of labour and social security or, failing this, an official from his Ministry, to be specially responsible for the settlement of collective disputes or of a collective dispute within the territorial competence of a given inspector of labour and social security.

The Minister of Labour and Social Security shall in all cases appoint by order an inspector of labour and social security or, failing this, an official from his Ministry, to settle collective disputes affecting the whole national territory or involving the territory of two or more regional inspectorates of labour and social security.

235. The competent inspector of labour and social security or, in default, the official specially appointed, shall convoke the parties within the 48 hours following notification of the collective dispute, unless the parties are covered by a collective agreement providing for special conciliation procedure, or in the 48 hours following notice of the failure of such procedure.

If one of the parties fails to appear, the conciliator shall issue a second convocation within a time limit not exceeding two days, without prejudice to such party's liability to a fine imposed by the competent court on the basis of a report drawn up by the Minister of Labour and Social Security, the amount of which shall be fixed under section 471, subsection 15, of the Penal Code.

The conciliator shall have the widest powers in obtaining information respecting the economic situation of the undertakings and the social circumstances of the workers involved in the dispute.

For this purpose he may make any inquiries concerning undertakings and trade unions and require the parties to produce any documents for information of an accounting or financial nature likely to be of assistance to him in investigating the dispute. Such investigation may be entrusted by the arbitrator to qualified persons such as approved accountancy experts.

The parties shall submit to the conciliator a statement of the case and any observations they may think fit to make.

They shall also be obliged to state the domicile of their choice for the purposes of the case ; such domicile shall be in the same place as one of the regional inspectorates of labour and social security, for the purpose of receiving, if necessary, notification of convocations referred to in the preceding sections.

The written report of conciliation or non-conciliation shall be drawn up immediately at the same meeting, and shall be signed forthwith by the conciliator and parties.

236. The conciliation agreement shall be immediately enforceable.

It shall be deposed at the secretariat of the labour court for the place where the regional inspectorate is situated, or in cases where there is a dispute as to territorial jurisdiction, with the secretariat of the labour court at Dakar.

It may subsequently be extended in accordance with the provisions of sections 87 et seq. of this Code.

237. If no agreement has been reached, the conciliator shall, within the following 48 hours, draw up a report on the state of the dispute and transmit it together with all the documents and information gathered by him to the Minister of Labour and Social Security. The report shall indicate the points on which it has been impossible to reach an agreement.

A copy of the report, indicating the date on which the original was sent to the competent Minister, shall be given to the parties without delay.

### Division II.   Arbitration

238. Within the eight days following the transmission of the conciliator's report, the Minister of Labour and Social Security shall notify the parties in writing, at the domicile chosen by them for the purpose of the case, if he decides to submit the dispute to arbitration, being of the opinion that a strike or lockout would adversely affect public order or be contrary to the public interest.

239. The Minister of Labour and Social Security shall appoint an arbitrator within the two days following his decision to submit the collective dispute to the arbitration procedure.

Any of the following may be appointed as arbitrator : an inspector of labour and social security or an official of the Ministry of Labour's department (provided that neither of them shall have been involved in the conciliation procedure) or a person chosen from a panel set up for this purpose each year by joint order of the Minister of Labour and Social Security and the Minister of Justice on a recommendation from the Director-General of Labour and Social Security.

The panel shall be composed of persons chosen on account of their moral authority and their competence in economic and social matters.

The arbitrator chosen from the panel set up as prescribed above shall not be a person who has participated in the attempt at conciliation, nor a person who has any direct interest in the dispute.

The report and the file established by the conciliator shall be transmitted to the arbitrator together with a copy of the decision appointing him.

240. Within 48 hours of reception of the above documents the arbitrator shall convoke the parties by notice addressed to the domicile chosen by them.

He shall hear the parties and make any investigations which may be necessary, having the powers prescribed in section 235 above.

The arbitrator shall observe professional secrecy respecting all documents entrusted to him.

The arbitrator shall not give a decision on any matters other than those contained in the written report of failure to reach conciliation or on matters which, being the result of events which took place later than the date on which the said report was drawn up, are a direct consequence of the current dispute.

He shall make an award within the ten days following receipt of the file and shall notify the parties by giving them a copy of the same, with a further copy for the Director-General of Labour and Social Security, to whom he shall return the file.

The award shall state the reasons on which it is based; it shall be immediately executory unless there is an appeal.

The award shall indicate the date on which it is to come into operation; it may have retroactive effect, but not further than the date on which the dispute was brought to the notice of the competent authority.

The award shall be immediately transmitted to the secretary of the competent labour court according to section 236 above. Unless it is appealed against, it may be extended in accordance with the provisions of sections 87 et seq. of this Code.

241. An appeal may be brought against the arbitration award.

The appeal shall be brought by the parties by written declaration submitted to the arbitrator within 48 hours following notification of the award.

242. The award appealed against shall be submitted to an arbitration board composed as follows : the First President of the Court of Appeal (chairman on the arbitration board), a judge of the Court of Appeal nominated by the First President, an official appointed by the Minister of Labour and Social Security (such an official shall not have been involved either in the conciliation or the arbitration proceedings), and two persons appointed by the Minister of Labour and Social Security from the panel of arbitrators provided for in section 239 of this Code.

The appeal shall be brought before the arbitration board for collective labour disputes by written declaration from the Director-General of Labour and Social Security, who shall transmit without delay the complete file of the case.

The arbitration board shall issue an award not later than the end of the month during which the file is thus transmitted.

It shall decide points on which no settlement could be reached during the attempt at conciliation and during the proceedings before the arbitrator (as set out in the conciliator's report or the arbitrator's award) or on points which arose after the above documents were drawn up or after an appeal was lodged against the arbitrator's award, but which are a direct consequence of the dispute concerned.

The arbitration board shall have the widest powers of investigation. It may carry out any additional inquiries.

The assessors on the arbitration board shall observe professional secrecy with respect to documents submitted to them and to the oral proceedings.

The award of the arbitration board shall be submitted without delay to the Director-General of Labour and Social Security, who shall immediately notify the parties.

The award shall be immediately enforceable. It shall not have retroactive effect.

The Director-General of Labour and Social Security shall transmit the award to the secretariat of the competent labour court according to section 236 above.

The award may be extended in accordance with the provisions of sections 87 et seq. of this Code.

No appeal may be made against the award other than an appeal to the Supreme Court within the time limits and subject to the formalities and conditions prescribed in Ordinance No. 60-17 of 3 September 1960, to promulgate the Basic Act respecting the Supreme Court.

243. The arbitrator and arbitration board shall decide on grounds of law in the case of disputes concerning the interpretation of laws, regulations, collective agreements or collective and other agreements in force.

They shall decide on grounds of equity all other disputes, particularly when the dispute concerns wages and conditions of work not prescribed by laws, regulations, collective agreements and other agreements in force, and disputes concerning the making and revision of clauses of collective agreements and other agreements.

Where the conciliation agreement, the arbitrator's award or the award of the arbitration board concerns the interpretation of the stipulations of a collective agreement respecting wages or conditions of work, the said agreement or award shall have the same effect as a collective labour agreement and may be subject to the same extension procedure.

Conciliation agreements, the arbitrator's award and awards of the arbitration boards shall be immediately inserted in the Official Gazette and posted up in the offices of the inspectorates of labour and social security concerned as well as in the workplace where the dispute arose.

244. Conciliation and arbitration procedure shall be free of charge. The rates for repayment of the costs of the procedure, *inter alia*, the costs of the travelling expenses of the conciliators, arbitrators, and members of the arbitration board, loss of wages and salaries, and experts' fees shall be fixed by decree.

245. A lockout or strike shall be lawful only if the Minister of Labour and Social Security has informed the parties in the manner prescribed in section 238 of this Act that he does not intend to submit the collective dispute to the arbitration procedure, or if he fails to so inform the parties within the eight days following the transfer of the conciliator's report.

246. A lockout or strike commenced in contravention of the provisions of section 245 shall render those responsible liable to the following penalties :
 (1) in the case of employers : payment of wages to the worker for the days lost ;
 (2) in the case of workers : loss of entitlement to compensation in lieu of notice and to damages for breach of contract ;
 (3) in the case of employers, by judgment of a court of first instance, given on an application made by the President of the Council : for a minimum period of two years, ineligibility for membership of a chamber of commerce, and a ban on participation in the work of the Economic and Social Council or an advisory committee or board for labour, manpower or social security or an arbitration board, or participation in any way in a contract for public works or supply on behalf of the State or a public body.

Appendix III

# LIST OF LEGAL TEXTS PUBLISHED
# IN THE ILO LEGISLATIVE SERIES

*Congo (Brazzaville)*
   Labour Code (Extracts) :  L.S. 1964 — Congo (Bra.) 1

*Congo (Léopoldville) (Kinshasa)*
   Legislative Ordinance No. 250, respecting collective labour agreements :
   L.S. 1963 — Congo (Léo.) 1
   Legislative Ordinance No. 122, respecting industrial relations : L.S.
   1964 — Congo (Léo.) 1

*Ethiopia*
   Labour Relations Decree 1962 :  L.S. 1962 — Eth. 1–A
   Civil Code 1960 (Extracts) :  L.S. 1962 — Eth. 1–B

*Gabon*
   Labour Code — L.S. 1962 — Gab. 1

*Ghana*
   Industrial Relations Act 1958 :  L.S. 1958 — Ghana 1
   Industrial Relations (Amendment) Act 1959 :  L.S. 1959 — Ghana 1

*Guinea*
   Labour Code :  L.S. 1960 — Gui. 1

*Ivory Coast*
   Labour Code (Extracts) :  L.S. 1964 — I.C. 1
   Decree No. 65–133 on collective disputes :  L.S. 1965 — I.C. 3

*Kenya*
   Regulation of Wages and Conditions of Employment Ordinance, 1951 :
   L.S. 1951 — Ken. 1
   Trade Disputes Act 1965 :  L.S. 1965 — Ken. 1

*Malagasy Republic*
   Labour Code :  L.S. 1960 — Mad. 1

*Mali*

Labour Code : L.S. 1962 — Mali 1

*Mauritania*

Labour Code : L.S. 1963 — Mau. 1

*Senegal*

Labour Code (Extracts) : L.S. 1962 — Sen. 2–B

*Somalia*

Labour Code : L.S. 1958 — It. Som. 1

*Southern Rhodesia*

Industrial Conciliation Act 1959 : L.S. 1959 — S.R. 1
Industrial Conciliation Amendment Act 1964 : L.S. 1964 — S.R. 1

*Sudan*

Trade Disputes Act 1960 : L.S. 1960 — Sud. 1

*Tanzania*

Trade Disputes (Settlement) Act 1962 : L.S. 1962 — Tan. 1

*Uganda*

Trades Disputes (Arbitration and Settlement) Ordinance, 1949 : L.S. 1949 — Ug. 1
Trades Disputes (Arbitration and Settlement) (Amendment) Ordinance, 1950 : L.S. 1950 — Ug. 1
Minimum Wages Advisory Boards and Wages Councils Ordinance, 1957 : L.S. 1957 — Ug. 1

*Zambia*

Trade Unions and Trade Disputes Ordinance, 1949 : L.S. 1949 — N.R. 1
Trade Unions and Trade Disputes (Amendment) Ordinance, 1958 : L.S. 1959 — N.R. 2
Industrial Conciliation Ordinance, 1949 : L.S. 1949 — N.R. 2
Industrial Conciliation (Amendment) Ordinance, 1958 : L.S. 1959 — N.R. 1

*Former French Territories*

Labour Code (Overseas Territories) : L.S. 1952 — Fr. 5
Labour Code (Overseas Territories) (Amendments) : L.S. 1955 — Fr. 3

# INDEX

Accidents, industrial, *see* Social benefits
Aleksandrov, N. G., vii n.
Arbitration, 61–63, 79, 149–52. *See also* Conciliation
Association Inter-professionnelle de L'Afrique tropicale, 44

Benefits in kind, 105–6
Berg, Elliott, 28 n., 38 n.
Brazzaville, *see* Congo

Cameroon
  *Code du Travail* (1952), 73
  collective agreements introduced, 9
  coverage, 15
  trade unions, 27
  wages, 78
  workers' representatives, 77
Central African Republic
  coverage, 13–14
  employment, 89 n.
  procedure, 75
Centre National du Patronat français, 43, 44
Chad
  *Code du Travail* (1952), 73
  coverage, 14
  state employment, 5
Check-off, 31, 83, 84–85, 86
Clothing grants, 106
*Code du Travail* (1952), 35, 39, 68–80, 93, 101, 105, 107, 114, 120, 126
Collective agreements
  content, 81–112
  duration, 117–19
  effects and sanction of, 119–23
  employment, 89–98
  free discussion, 126
  grievances, 123–30
  groups concerned, 114–17
  holidays, 110–12
  implementation, 113–30
  social benefits, 106–10
  trade union rights, 83–88
  wages, 98–106
  work hours, 110–12
Collective bargaining in English-speaking countries, 48–68
  bargaining machinery, 55–61
  development, 48
  disputes, settlement of, 61–68
  level of negotiations, 53–55
  recognition of trade unions, 49–53
  strikes, 64–68
Collective bargaining in French-speaking countries, 68–80
  *Code du Travail*, 68–80
  Labour Inspectorate, 76
  legislative evolution since independ-
  strikes, 72          [ence, 73–76
  theory and practice, 76–80

Commissions of Inquiry, 62
Conciliation, 61–63, 126–30, 147–149
Confédération des Travailleurs Chrétiens, 27–28
Confédération Générale du Travail, 27–28
Confederation of Believing Workers, Pan African, 28
Congo (Brazzaville)
  agreements, drafting of, 73
  coverage, 14
  procedure, 74, 75
  sick pay, 107
Congo (Kinshasa)
  coverage, 23
  Sabena Airlines, 23
Conspiracy and Protection of Property Act (1875), 65
Coverage, 8 ff.

Dahomey
  *Code du Travail* (1952), 73
  coverage, 11
  wages, 118 n.
de Vyver, F. T., xviii n.
Doctor, K. C., 1 n., 6 n., 10 n.
Douty, H. M., 38 n.

Employers, 36–45
  associations and organisations, x–xiii, 41–45
  governments as, xii, 37–39
  private, 40
Employment
  accident, 93
  apprenticeship, 90
  changes in contract, 91
  collective dismissals, 94–95
  compensation, 96
  discipline, 92
  initial, 89
  legal aspects, 89–98
  long-service gratuities, 98
  maternity, 93
  notice of dismissal, 95
  probationary period, 89
  promotion, 91
  sickness, 93
  suspension of contract, 93–94
  termination, 94
  termination grant, 97
Ethiopia
  collective agreements as binding, 122
  coverage, 23
  decree of 1962, 51
  extension of agreements, 116
  Labour Relations Board, 62
  period of agreements, 118
  strikes, 66–67

155

Food grants, 106
French Equatorial Africa, 9, 27
French West Africa, 9, 27, 43

Gabon
    coverage, 14–15
    procedure, 74, 75, 76
Galenson, W., 28 n.
Gallis, Hans, 1 n., 6 n., 10 n.
Gambia, coverage, 22
General Union of Workers of Black
    Africa, 28
Ghana
    apprenticeship, 90
    bargaining basis, 54
    changes in employment contract, 91
    check-off, 84–85
    collective agreement as contract,
        121–2
    coverage, 20–21
    dismissals from employment, 94–95,
        98
    extension of agreements, 116
    holidays, 111, 112 n.
    Industrial Relations Act (1958), 39,
        51, 56, 59, 66, 114, 116, 122 n.
    period of agreements, 118
    sick pay, 107–8, 109
    strikes, 65–66
    trade unions, 24, 25, 26, 27, 34, 84–
        85, 87 n.
    transport agreement (1960), 88 n.
    union contributions, 31
    wages, 100 n., 103 n., 104 n., 105 n.
    work schedules, 92
Gonidec, P. F., 27 n., 28 n.
    and Kirsch, 69 n., 71 n., 120 n., 128 n.
Governments as employers, xii, 37–39
Guillebaud, C. W., 41 n.
Guinea
    agreements, drafting of, 73
    arbitration, 79
    Code of 1960, 128 n.
    coverage, 13
    procedure, 74
    state employment, 5
    trade unions, 28, 34

Holidays
    annual, 110–11
    public, 111
    special leave, 111–12
Housing benefits, 105–6

International Confederation of Free
    Trade Unions, 28
International Labour Code, 52
Ivory Coast
    coverage, 11
    employment, 89, 96
    procedure, 73 n., 75
    wages, 100 n., 105 n.

Joint Industrial Councils, 58

Kenya
    accrued benefits, preservation of,
        118 n.
    agriculture, 54, 101, 118 n.
    check-off, 84–85
    Coffee Growers' Association, 41
    collective agreements as binding, 122
    concept of essential service, 61 n.
    conciliation, 62
    coverage, 17–18
    dismissals from employment, 98
    disputes, settlement of, 62
    employment policy, 134–5
    extension of agreements, 117
    food grants, 106
    food-processing industries, 55 n.
    Industrial Charter (1962), 52, 80 n.,
        131–7
    industrial courts, 62
    insurance, 54
    intimidation, 136
    joint consultation, 136
    labour force, 5
    petroleum industry, 90 n.
    probationary employment, 90 n.
    redundancy, 95 n., 134
    sick pay, 107, 108 n., 109
    Singer Company, 98 n., 100 n., 108 n.
    state employment, 5
    strikes, 66–67, 135
    Trade Disputes Act (1965), 66, 117
    trade unions, 25 n., 27, 84–85
    wages, 100 n., 101, 101 n., 103 n.,
        104 n., 106
Kinshasa, *see* Congo

Labour force
    Africanisation, 102
    public sector, 6
    racial composition, 7–8
    size and distribution, 1–5
Léopoldville (Kinshasa), *see* Congo
Liberia
    coverage, 22
    Labour Practices Review Board, 62
    wages, 101 n.

Madagascar
    collective agreements introduced in, 9
    holidays, 111
    procedure, 73 n., 74, 75
    trade unions, 27
Malagasy Republic, coverage, 15
Malawi
    awards, legal position, 64
    coverage, 20
    negotiated agreements as binding, 122
    period of notice (agreements), 119 n.
    trade unions and political parties,
        86 n.

Mali
    arbitration, 79
    check-off agreements, 31
    coverage, 12
    Federation of (1959–60), 10
    procedure, 74, 75, 76
    state employment, 5
    trade unions, 28
Maternity, *see* Social benefits
Mauritania
    coverage, 13
    procedure, 75, 76
    sick pay, 107
    suspension of employment, 94
    trade unions, 27
    wages, 99 n., 105 n.
Medical care, *see* Social benefits
Meynaud, Jean, 28 n.

Niger
    coverage, 11
    procedure, 74, 75
Nigeria
    bargaining pattern, 54
    changes in employment contract, 91
    collective agreements, procedure, 82 n.
    coverage, 21
    holidays, 111, 112
    provident funds, 109 n.
    Shell Company, 87 n., 96 n., 97,
        110 n.
    sick pay, 109
    termination grants, 97
    Total Oil Company, 85 n., 110 n.
    trade unions, 25, 26, 85, 87, 88 n.
    wages, 105 n.
    Whitley Councils, 60
    work hours, 110
Nyasaland, trade unions, 25 n.

Organisation of Employers' Federations,
    42
Oubangui-Chari, 13
Overseas Employers' Federation, 42

Pension funds, *see* Social benefits
Phelps-Brown, E. H., vii n.
Preconditions for development, ix–x
Process, xiii
Provident funds, *see* Social benefits

Racial discrimination, 7, 102, 134
Reynaud, J.-D., ix n.
Rhodesia
    Collective agreements as binding, 122
    labour force in, 5
    Northern, copper mining industry,
        7, 16
        European workers in, 7
        trade unions, 25 n.
    Southern, coverage, 19–20
        extension of agreements, 116
        industrial courts, 62, 116

Roberts, B. C., xii n., 16 n., 26 n.,
    36 n., 37 n., 42 n., 61 n.
Ross, Philip, 52 n.

Salah-Bey, Amine, 28 n.
Scope and content, xvi
Sellier, F., ix n.
Senegal
    arbitration, 79, 149–52
    conciliation, 147–9
    coverage, 10–11
    employers' associations, 43
    food for workers, 106
    Labour Code, 80 n., 138–53
    labour disputes, 144–52
    procedure, 74, 75, 76
    strikes, 152
    trade unions, 27
    wages, 100 n.
    workers' representatives, 77
Sick pay, *see* Social benefits
Sierra Leone
    apprenticeship, 90
    compensation, 96 n.
    coverage, 21–22
    extension of agreements, 116, 117
    holidays, 110 n.
    legality of agreements, 122
    Shell Company, 103 n., 107 n., 108 n.
    sick pay, 107 n., 108 n.
    trade unions, 25, 27
    Trade Unions Act, 52 n.
    wages, 103 n., 105 n.
    Wages Boards Ordinance, 56
Skilled workers, 5–6
Social benefits, 106–10
    accidents, 108
    maternity, 108
    medical care, 109
    pension funds, 109
    provident funds, 109
    sickness, 107–8
Somalia
    agricultural agreement (1962), 125 n.
    coverage, 23
    wages, 103 n.
Strikes, 61, 64–68, 72, 135, 152
Sudan
    Act of 1960, 51
    clothing grants, 106
    collective agreements as binding,
        122
    coverage, 23
    ' Gezira Scheme ', 23
    holidays, 111 n., 112
    Shell Company, 94, 103
    strikes, 66–67
    suspension of employment, 94
    wages, 103
Syndicat des Commercants, Importa-
    teurs-Exportateurs, 43

Tanganyika
concept of essential service, extent
of, 61 n.
trade unions, 25 n.
Tanzania
Act of 1962, 66
Act of 1964, 59 n.
agriculture, centralised bargaining in,
54
arbitration, 62, 67 n.
check-off, 84–85
coverage, 18–19
disputes, settlement of, 127 n.
labour force in, 5
negotiated agreements as binding, 122
Plantation Workers' Union, 41
sick pay, 109
Sisal Growers' Association, 19, 41
state employment, 5
strikes, 65–66
Trade Disputes Ordinance (1962),
116 n.
trade unions, 24, 41
union contributions, 31
Togo
*Code du Travail* (1952), 73
coverage, 11
wages, 78 n.
Trade unions, 24–35
access to employees, 86
activities in plant, 86
Cameroon, 27
check-off agreements, 31, 83, 84–85
closed shop, 85
development, x–xiii
exercise of rights, 83–88
French Equatorial Africa, 27
French West Africa, 27
future of, 32
Ghana, 24, 25, 26, 27
Guinea, 28
Kenya, 25 n., 27
leadership, 32–33
Madagascar, 27, 28
Mali, 28, 31
Mauritania, 27
membership instability, 30–31
Nigeria, 25, 26, 34
Northern Rhodesia, 25 n.
Nyasaland, 25 n.
officers, leave for, 87
recognition of, 47, 49–53, 85–86,
133–4
Senegal, 27
shop stewards, 87
Sierra Leone, 25, 27
strength, 30
structure and collective bargaining,
English-speaking countries, 25–27
structure and collective bargaining,
French-speaking countries, 27–30
Tanganyika, 25 n.

Trade unions (*contd.*)
Tanzania, 24, 27
Uganda, 25 n.
Zambia, 27
Zanzibar, 25 n.
Trade unions and Trade Disputes Act
(1927), 67
Turner, H. A., xviii n., 7

Uganda
accrued benefits, preservation of,
118 n.
awards, legal position, 64
coverage, 18
employment, 89 n., 95 n.
motor trade, 95 n.
plantations, 54, 88 n.
Shell Company, 95 n., 105 n.
trade unions, 25 n., 86
wages, 100 n., 105 n.
Union Générale des Travailleurs
d'Afrique Noire, 28
Union Intersyndicale d'Entreprises et
d'Industrie de l'A.O.F., 43
United States, check-off in, 84
union membership as condition of
employment, 85
Upper Volta
agreements, drafting of, 73
coverage, 11–12
procedure, 74, 75, 76

Voluntary persuasion, 47

Wages, 77–78, 98–106
displacement allowances, 104–5
equal pay for equal work, 101
extra, for special jobs, 103–4
increases, and length of service, 101–2
job classification, 99–101
overtime, 103
productivity standards and, 103
*See also* Benefits in kind
Wages Boards, 56–58
Wages Councils, 56, 58
Webb, S. and B., vii n., 37 n.
Whitley Councils, 22, 38–39, 60
Work hours, 110–12

Zambia
closed shop, 85
collective agreements as binding, 122
copper-mining industry, 41, 54, 56 n.,
59, 85, 100 n., 109 n., 119
coverage, 16–17
European workers, 8
extension of agreements, 116
medical care, 109
period of notice (agreements), 119 n.
trade unions, 27, 85
wages, 100 n., 104 n.
Zanzibar, trade unions, 25 n.